SUNDERLAND GREATS

SUNDERLAND GREATS

PAUL HETHERINGTON

Foreword
BOB MURRAY

SPORTSPRINT PUBLISHING
EDINBURGH

ISBN 0 85976 266 1

Phototypeset by Beecee Typesetting Services
Printed in Great Britain by Bell & Bain Ltd., Glasgow

Foreword

Every word written on Sunderland Football Club is of great interest to me, whether it is a newspaper article or a major work such as this book *Sunderland Greats.*

The club has certainly had its share of great and charismatic players. Some of them are included in this book which I am sure not only Sunderland, but true football supporters in general, will find of great interest.

During the 34 years I have been watching the fortunes of the Red and Whites, my first idol was Charlie Hurley, a man I would walk to the ends of the earth to watch. Brian Clough, so short a time at Sunderland, but embroidered on my memory for life. Jim Montgomery — what a loyal servant to the club. All these and many other players have been fully worthy of credit.

I am both delighted and honoured, therefore, to pen the Foreword to this book, written by someone who also cares about this great club. I have enjoyed a good working relationship with Paul Hetherington and know he will have tackled the task with comprehensive thought. I am therefore happy to give the official blessing of the club to this work.

Sunderland Football Club is the focal point for a million people, it affects their lives and is so vital to the area. My interest in the club is neither professional nor business, it is purely personal. Or could it be that I am just in love with the club?

The club has come through many years of difficulty, but I believe we have made excellent progress in the last two years and created a foundation on which to build. We can now all work together to bring about a regeneration of both the club and the area. Football is also troubled in general, but this is nothing new: 'He longs for only two things — bread and the big match' (Juvenal, *Of the Citizen of These Days, circa* AD 100).

I also hope for togetherness and friendship in the game and feel deeply for the professionals, which reminds me of a quote from John F. Kennedy at his inauguration address as President: 'Victory has a thousand fathers, but defeat is an orphan.'

The task before us at the club is so great that I believe very few have a true understanding of the work in hand. However, my main ambition as Chairman is that one day you will have yet another team of Greats to compete at the top level and bring success.

With all best wishes,
BOB MURRAY
CHAIRMAN
SUNDERLAND AFC

Acknowledgements

My sincere thanks to everyone who gave up their time to assist me with this book, in particular the players whom I interviewed and Bob Stokoe, who I know conducted interviews of his own as part of his thorough approach in picking a Sunderland post-war team.

A special word of gratitude to Sunderland chairman Bob Murray, for supplying the Foreword in addition to his general support.

I must also acknowledge the contribution of my dad, who 'suffered' on the Roker beat for 22 years when covering the fortunes of the club for the Newcastle *Evening Chronicle* and loved every minute of it — particularly 1973!

Photographs were kindly provided by the Newcastle Chronicle and Journal Ltd., Dennis Tueart — from his personal collection — and the *Sunday Sun's* Chief Photographer, Eric Burns, who also took the cover picture.

Contents

CHAPTER ONE

Introduction

The Glory Days

Sunderland's glory days were pre-war, or to be precise, pre-wars.

Before World War Two the club won the First Division Championship in 1936, were runners-up in 1923 and 1935 and F.A. Cup winners in 1937.

But while that superb side of the 1930s, which featured superstars of that era like Raich Carter and Bobby Gurney, was something special, Sunderland enjoyed most of their success before the First World War, when they were known as the Team Of All The Talents.

The club, formed as Sunderland and District Teachers' Association in 1879, were elected to the First Division in 1890 and within five years had won the Championship three times — in 1892, '93 and '95.

Further Division One title triumphs followed in 1902 and 1913, when defeat by Aston Villa in the F.A. Cup Final prevented the club achieving the coveted double. They have never come as close since.

And during a period when Sunderland were the premier club in the country, they were also runners-up in the First Division in 1894, 1898 and 1901.

How times have changed!

The great star of Sunderland's team between 1911 and 1925 was Charlie Buchan, whose famous monthly football magazine made him a household name with football fans half a century later.

Buchan scored more league goals for the club than any other player, with 209, plus another 15 in F.A. Cup-ties. He was the first player to score five goals in a league match for the club, a feat performed against Liverpool in 1919 in a 7-0 win.

His achievement was later equalled by Gurney in 1935 (a 7-2 win against Bolton) and Nick Sharkey, the only player to do so in a competitive match since the Second World War. His five came in a 7-1 victory against Norwich in 1962.

Gurney went on to set an overall club scoring record of 228 goals — 205 of them in the league.

Buchan was succeeded by another great goal scorer — Dave Halliday. His haul of 43 in season 1928-29 is the highest achieved by a Sunderland player in one campaign.

Sunderland's biggest victories were also achieved in the early days — 11-1 against Fairfield in the first round of the F.A. Cup in 1895 and 9-1 at Newcastle in a First Division match in 1908.

That victory at St. James's Park was some achievement as Newcastle won the Championship that season, with Sunderland finishing third.

Sunderland, who turned professional in 1886 and became a limited company in 1906, played at five different grounds before setting up home at Roker Park in 1898.

They started off at Blue House Field, Hendon and later played at Ashbrooke, the site of Cooper Street, Abbs Field, Fulwell and Newcastle Road.

The record attendance at Roker was established in 1933, when 75,118 watched an F.A. Cup sixth round replay against Derby County.

It's a measure of Sunderland's standing in the game before the Second World War that even now only five clubs have achieved more League Championship wins than Sunderland's six — Liverpool, Everton, Arsenal, Manchester United and Aston Villa.

Sunderland's greatest post-war moment — Ian Porterfield (no. 10) strikes the winner against Leeds in the 1973 F.A. Cup Final.

Post-war struggle

One year stands out in Sunderland's post-war history — 1973.

It was the year Sunderland, then in the Second Division, achieved the most romantic of F.A. Cup victories, against Leeds United at Wembley.

But that solitary major success since the Second World War — and the wonderful memories it still has for those who witnessed a remarkable run to the final — also underlines just how depressing an era it has been for the club.

For a club which won the League Championship six times before 1939 and which has remained one of the best supported in the country, one F.A. Cup win since 1945 is a pathetic record.

Sunderland's supporters are long suffering. They have had to endure five relegations, with the last in 1987 — to the Third Division for the first time in the club's 108-year history — being the most humiliating of the lot.

But while Sunderland's glory days were before the

Second World War, there have still been great players at Roker Park since then — and I'm not just referring to the opposition!

That's what this book is all about — Sunderland's Greats of the post-war era.

I've picked out eight — including three members of the Wembley-winning side — and also selected a current player who could be the next Roker Great. More of those players later.

It must be said that it was an enormously difficult task limiting the total to just eight. My Sunderland-watching days started in season 1959-60 and, therefore, I have included only one player before then — Len Shackleton, who is regarded as Roker's greatest post-war star in the same way that the late Jackie Milburn is thought of at Newcastle and Wilf Mannion at Middlesbrough.

No book on Sunderland's outstanding post-war players would be complete without Shack, whom I knew as a Press Box colleague during his days as a football writer.

The criteria for the players I selected were outstanding ability and service to the club. Sadly, the greatness was confirmed, in some cases, when they moved on to other clubs because of Sunderland's lack of success.

Literally hundreds of players have failed to make Roker's great eight, including some who were not only particular favourites of mine, but also personal friends.

It is only right, though, that I also pay tribute to some of them for their contribution to the club's cause.

Jim Baxter, who joined Sunderland from Glasgow Rangers for £72,500 in May, 1965, was one of the few genuinely world-class players to play for Sunderland. He gave some wonderful performances, but his great days were behind him when he arrived at Roker, unlike some of the outstanding home-produced youngsters who left the club.

Northern Ireland internationals Martin Harvey and Billy Bingham — now manager of his country — were outstanding servants in addition to being class players.

We've won the cup. Manager Bob Stokoe raises the most famous trophy in football.

Billy Elliott, an England international, is in a similar category and later served the club as coach and manager.

Centre forward Charlie Fleming scored 71 goals in 122 league and cup appearances in the middle to late 1950s and one of his predecessors, Welsh international Trevor Ford, had a similar record with 70 in 117 games.

On the subject of scorers, Bryan 'Pop' Robson and Gary Rowell will always be special in the eyes of Sunderland supporters.

Rowell equalled Shackleton's post-war scoring record of exactly 100 goals and Robson was signed by the club no fewer than three times, twice from West Ham and once from Chelsea as a player-coach.

Robson had the most extraordinary Sunderland career. It seemed the club could never quite make up its mind whether he was wanted at Roker or not. His record, though, gave the most overpowering evidence that he should never have been shown the door, yet it happened three times.

Two managers — Bob Stokoe and Ken Knighton — bought and sold him and Len Ashurst gave Robson his exit ticket in a car-park meeting when he was player-coach after Alan Durban had brought him back to the club.

But Stokoe, Knighton and Ashurst all had to thank him for his goals and he specialised in the ones that were of a vital nature. Twice he helped shoot Sunderland to promotion, in 1976 under Stokoe and four years later when Knighton was in charge.

Pop scored one of Sunderland's goals — his 15th of the season — in the 2-1 defeat of Bolton Wanderers on April 24, 1976 which clinched promotion to the First Division in front of a Roker crowd of 51,983.

In season '79-80, he hit the target 22 times and in the penultimate game of the season, headed a brilliant and precious equaliser at Cardiff City when the promotion dream was in danger of fading.

Robson didn't just score goals to take Sunderland into the First Division, he also did it to keep the club there.

In the final match of season '83-84, he played at Leicester at the age of 38 years, 128 days — making him the oldest player in Sunderland's history — and scored in a 2-0 win which ensured the club's safety.

That was the season he was player-coach and showed he hadn't lost his scoring instincts with three goals in seven First Division appearances.

In all, Robson made 164 League and Cup appearances for Sunderland and spiced them with 67 goals. He was the player who came closest to challenging my final selection of eight.

There were many other candidates, like Willie Watson — an England international at both cricket and football — and Wembley-winning skipper Bobby Kerr.

But I eventually selected the following eight — Jimmy Montgomery, Dave Watson, Dennis Tueart, Shackleton, Charlie Hurley, Stan Anderson, Brian Clough and Colin Todd plus one for the future — Marco Gabbiadini.

Monty — who holds the club appearances record —

Street life. Fawcett Street in Sunderland town centre on the day they brought back the cup.

Watson and Tueart were the three members of the '73 side I selected. In addition to their contribution to that success, they were also brilliant individuals who weren't out of place in the highest class.

Shack, the Clown Prince of Soccer, is still the post-war player the majority of people throughout the country would name if they had to pick one Sunderland star.

Hurley was another automatic choice. Not only was he an inspiring captain and crowd favourite, but he also came closer than any other Sunderland player to winning the coveted Footballer of the Year award, when he was runner-up to Bobby Moore in 1964.

King Charlie's special place in Sunderland's history was confirmed during the club's centenary celebrations in 1979, when he topped a poll to find the greatest player in those 100 years.

Anderson was part of a famous half-back line, as they

were known in those days, with Hurley and Jimmy McNab, before losing his place to Northern Ireland international Harvey, who also had the distinction of displacing Danny Blanchflower in his country's international team.

Not many players win England caps while with a Second Division club. That is still very much the case now, but Anderson managed it during a Sunderland career of 12 years which saw him establish what was then an appearances record of 447 games.

In contrast, his former team-mate Clough made only 74 League and Cup appearances for Sunderland, but hit a staggering 63 goals.

Clough's brilliant playing days were wrecked by injury. It meant an earlier start to an equally eye-catching managerial career which, sadly and foolishly from Sunderland's point of view, has not included a period at Roker Park.

One of his managerial masterstrokes was to sign my final Roker great — Todd — for Derby County. Like Tueart, he became an England international after leaving Sunderland, for whom he was brilliant in the First Division even when only 17.

Three of my eight — Todd, Tueart and Watson — were sold by Sunderland before they reached their peak.

That's a trend which has continued at the club during the 1980s until the arrival of Bob Murray as chairman. He is committed to retaining Sunderland's outstanding youngsters and that is a welcome step.

Sunderland have been powerless to prevent the departure of some players through freedom of contract and there have been other understandable reasons for transfers.

A worrying financial situation, using the proceeds of a sale to finance other deals and the feeling that an unhappy player is better away from the club have all been used as explanations for departures.

But it is also true that a club can't expect to be successful if it continues to sell its best players. Sunderland have been guilty of that.

The homecoming — Sunderland's open-topped bus ride with the F.A. Cup.

I remain convinced that the club's best chance of success in recent years was when Alan Durban was in charge of the side. It was a time of struggle, but at least it was First Division struggle.

It was one Sunderland were winning, too. Durban was building a side which was proving it could compete in the top flight and, as a young team, would have improved with the right additions — and it would only have taken a couple.

Durban was sacked because of a deteriorating relationship with chairman at the time Tom Cowie, his own stubbornness in rejecting a one-year contract extension which he considered to be an insult, and through a failure to make progress in cup competitions.

That would have sustained interest in the second half of seasons and also generated much-needed revenue. Sunderland, though, failed to clear the second hurdle of either the F.A. Cup or the League Cup during his three-year reign.

If he had remained in charge, members of his squad could have developed into Roker greats — players like Paul Bracewell, Barry Venison and Chris Turner, who was a realistic candidate in any case as the club's best goal-keeper since Montgomery.

It is significant that their departures took them to clubs of the stature of Everton, Liverpool and Manchester United, confirmation of their talent.

It is also significant that Durban's sacking in March, 1984 led to a decline in the club's fortunes which wasn't arrested until the arrival of a Durban old boy as manager — Denis Smith, his former centre-half at Stoke City.

By then, Sunderland's humiliation was complete. Their slide had taken them from the First Division to the Third, but Smith led the club back to the Second Division at the first attempt and a brighter era was underway at Roker.

Durban's successor — Len Ashurst — led Sunderland to Wembley in 1985 for the Milk Cup Final, but there was to be no repeat of '73. Norwich won a bitterly disappointing final 1-0 and relegation followed for Roker.

Ashurst was sacked to make way for Lawrie McMenemy, who failed miserably to live up to a reputation established through smooth success at Southampton.

Big Mac's Roker reign tarnished his polished image. The team he created took Sunderland out of the Second Division all right — but it was into the Third for the first time in the Club's history.

Stokoe was back at the club by then as caretaker manager after McMenemy had become the ninth Sunderland post-war boss to be sacked. But even he had run out of the sort of magic which transformed the club in '73.

With Knighton and his assistant Frank Clark also fired in 1981 after less than two seasons in charge — a decision which was harsh to say the least considering that they had won promotion to Division One at the first attempt — the last decade hasn't been the sort to produce Roker greats.

Of the players I have picked, only one manager had an involvement with all eight — Alan Brown, who had two periods in charge at Roker. He signed three of them — Hurley, Clough and Watson — and blooded another two, Montgomery and Tueart.

But while Anderson and Todd made the bulk of their Sunderland appearances as Brown players, Shackleton played only once for the man known as The Bomber, before hanging up his boots.

Shack was signed by Sunderland when the manager was Bill Murray, who also introduced Anderson to the Football League.

Hurley also played for George Hardwick and Ian McColl, who gave Todd his debut. Montgomery appeared for every manager from Brown to George Hardwick, to McColl, Brown again and Stokoe, who also had Watson and Tueart in his Sunderland side.

Every regular Roker observer over the years will have his or her own opinion of the post-war greats and I have no doubt that many will disagree with mine. What is certain, though, is that my eight have been special to the club, as their records prove.

Gabbiadini, the current idol of the Roker fans and a bargain buy by Smith at £80,000, might be about to join them.

CHAPTER TWO

Jimmy Montgomery

It was an easy decision to make Jimmy Montgomery the choice for the first chapter on the players who make up my Sunderland post-war greats.

After all, he was literally Sunderland's No. 1 for the most part of 14 years and is still the club's No. 1 for appearances. Monty made 615 starts in League, F.A. Cup, League Cup and European Cup-Winners' Cup matches. It's a record which will probably never be beaten.

That would be appropriate, because there were also times on the pitch when Montgomery was unbeatable.

One of them, of course, was the '73 Cup Final, when Monty carved his own niche in Wembley history. Midway through the second half, with Sunderland hanging onto the lead provided by Ian Porterfield's 31st-minute goal, Leeds seemed certain to equalise.

Paul Reaney's cross from the right was met by Trevor Cherry's diving header. Montgomery dived to his left to push the ball out, only for it to be met just six yards from goal by Peter Lorimer — the man regarded at the time as having the hardest shot in football.

The Scottish international instantly struck the ball towards a seemingly empty net, describing his shot as being hit 'hard and cleanly.' Monty's strength, however, had always been his reflexes and he threw himself into the path of the ball and managed to deflect it with his right hand onto the underside of the bar. When the ball bounced down on the right side of the line for Sunderland, full-back Dick Malone despatched it to safety.

As Monty's first save — from Cherry — had been made with his left hand, he had produced a one-two of

Airborne — Monty makes another breathtaking save.

devastating proportions to Leeds, the hottest of favourites to retain the trophy they had won the previous season against Arsenal.

Bob Stokoe's sprint across the pitch at the final whistle to hug his goalkeeper, told its own story. It was the manager's emotional way of saying: 'You've won us the Cup.'

Montgomery's acrobatic double save was one of the great moments in the history of F.A. Cup Finals and no-one realised that more at the time than Lorimer.

He said of his shot: 'I was certain it would be the goal which would set us up for the winner. I don't know where Jimmy came from. He was on the deck when I got in the shot.

'I just couldn't believe my eyes when his fist appeared from nowhere and the ball came out off the bar. I'll never forget that moment as long as I live.'

No-one with Sunderland connections who witnessed that example of Monty magic will forget it, either.

Yet until that double save, I felt during the match that Montgomery had looked uncomfortable at times and not at his most inspiring.

Wembley may have been his greatest moment, but it wasn't his greatest performance. And for that matter, Monty reckons it wasn't even the scene of his greatest save.

Montgomery recalls: 'I made a better save at Hull just two weeks before Wembley. It was a Second Division match which we won 2-0 — Billy Hughes and Vic Halom were the scorers — and even at the time I couldn't tell you which Hull player was involved.

'I just know that I had to scoop the ball out when a goal looked certain. It was a similar save to the one Gordon Banks made from Pele's header in the Brazil-England match in Mexico during the 1970 World Cup.

'That save at Hull was more difficult than the one I made at Wembley, and for that reason I would rate it as the best I made. It was a reflex save — all my best ones were. I was never as happy with the long-range efforts!'

Monty had countless brilliant games for Sunderland, but picks out his most memorable performance as easily as he nominates his best save.

It came early in his career — December 8, 1962 to be precise, at Leeds Road, Huddersfield. Monty was only 19 and those who witnessed his display in that Second Division match knew — if there was any doubt — that Sunderland had a very special goalkeeper.

The crowd of 21,260 who saw the match saw Huddersfield play brilliantly, particularly in the first half, yet lose 3-0. There was no score at half-time for one reason — Montgomery's heroics.

'It was a tremendous match and I can remember Len

White, the former Newcastle player, having a great game for Huddersfield. But I managed to stop everything they threw at me and we were happy to go in at half-time at 0-0,' says Monty.

'In the second half, we got an early goal and eventually won by a flattering scoreline. Brian Clough scored twice and George Mulhall got our other goal. It was a great result for us, and even though I played hundreds of games after that, I always regarded that performance at Huddersfield as my best,' Montgomery added.

Montgomery's great Sunderland career started on October 4, 1961 in a League Cup-tie at Roker Park against Walsall. He was five days short of his 18th birthday and was beaten twice that night, but still finished on the winning side.

Sunderland won 5-2, but he had to wait another four months before making his League debut against Derby County, who were defeated 2-1 at Roker.

Monty played in 11 of the next 12 matches, including a 3-0 derby win against Newcastle in front of a Roker crowd of 57,666. Sunderland lost only one of those games — 3-2 at Plymouth where they had to play with 10 men for the last half-hour after centre-half Dickie Rooks suffered a broken cheekbone.

That run established Montgomery as Sunderland's first-choice 'keeper in succession to the deposed Peter Wakeham. He was only 18 and had virtually leapfrogged the reserve side in going from the juniors to the first team.

He didn't miss a match for the next two seasons, which culminated in Sunderland winning promotion to the First Division with this regular line-up: Montgomery, Irwin, Ashurst, Harvey, Hurley, McNab, Usher, Herd, Sharkey, Crossan, Mulhall.

Cruelly, a hand injury prevented Monty being part of the club's return to Division One. Derek Forster, at 15 years and 185 days, became the youngest player in Sunderland's history when he deputised for the first three games.

Sunderland then signed Sandy McLaughlan from

Kilmarnock for £12,000 and he gave the fit-again Montgomery competition for the goalkeeper's jersey before Monty established himself as undisputed No. 1 midway through the following season.

Monty was a fixture in the side after that and experienced relegation in 1970, the Cup triumph and another promotion in 1976, when the Roker line-up was: Montgomery, Malone, Bolton, Towers, Ashurst, Moncur, Kerr, Train, Holden, Robson, Greenwood.

It's a further tribute to his talent that the closest he came to a full England cap was during a period of great struggle for the club. Monty was an England youth international and made six under-23 appearances, but didn't quite make the full national side.

The nearest he came was a Wembley match against France in March 1969, when he was reserve to the great Gordon Banks, who was declared fit shortly before the kick off — after being in doubt — to deprive Montgomery of that elusive cap.

In Sunderland's relegation year of 1970, Monty was named in England's World Cup 40, but didn't make the final squad which travelled to Mexico and remained the goalkeeper recognised throughout most of his playing career as the best uncapped 'keeper in the country.

But his cap certainly fitted at Roker Park. He could have joined Burnley as a boy, but returned to his native Wearside after a month at Turf Moor. They already had Colin McDonald, Adam Blacklaw and Jim Furnell in their goalkeeping ranks and the ambitious Montgomery felt he would have to wait longer for a senior chance than he was prepared to do.

At Sunderland, for whom he signed on October 10, 1960, he first overhauled Stan Anderson's appearances record and then Len Ashurst's.

He had a testimonial match against Newcastle in May, 1974 which drew a crowd of 29,625, and the last of his 615 League and Cup appearances for the club was in a 1-0 home defeat by Everton on October 2, 1976.

Montgomery was displaced just before his 33rd birthday by Barry Siddall, signed from Bolton Wanderers for £88,000. He played for Southampton on loan and then Birmingham City before Brian Clough — his former Sunderland team-mate — signed him for Nottingham Forest as cover for England No. 1, Peter Shilton.

Monty didn't make a League appearance for Forest, yet left the City Ground with a European Cup winners' medal. He was substitute 'keeper when Clough's side defeated Hamburg in the 1980 final in Madrid.

There was consolation, therefore, for the disappointment of having to leave Roker. It didn't just come at Forest, either.

Montgomery admits: 'I had three fabulous years at Birmingham. I made my debut against Derby County at the Baseball Ground in March, 1977 and saved a penalty from Charlie George in a 0-0 draw.

'I took over in goal from Dave Latchford, brother of the former England centre-forward, Bob. He was a popular and respected 'keeper at St. Andrew's and I needed to make a good impression straight away.

'That penalty save got my Birmingham career underway in the right manner and in my second season there, I won their Player of the Year award — pipping Trevor Francis. So I've got happy memories of Birmingham and I also had one good year at Forest — even though I wasn't picked for a League game.

'The only first-team game I played was in the County Cup against Notts County, but it was great being on the bench as cover for Peter Shilton in the European Cup-ties, and to finish up with a winners' medal was a real bonus at the end of my career — as was experiencing Cloughie's style of management.'

Actually, Monty's career wasn't quite over when he left Forest at the end of the 1979-80 season. He was to make one more move — back to Sunderland on a free transfer.

Ken Knighton, Sunderland's manager at the time, recruited him as cover, and while he didn't make another senior appearance for the club, he became youth team coach a year later.

But after just a year in the job, Knighton's successor — Alan Durban — told Montgomery that he was not being retained.

'It hurt to be told I wasn't wanted,' Monty admitted. 'I knew everyone at the club from the tea ladies upwards and it was hard to accept I was leaving Roker Park for the second time.

'What made it worse was that the juniors had a good season when I was with them. We reached the semi-final of the F.A. Youth Cup and only went out of the competition to a strong Manchester United side, which included Mark Hughes, Norman Whiteside and Graeme Hogg.

'We also finished third in the Northern Intermediate League that season and I helped bring through players like Barry Venison, Nick Pickering, Paul Atkinson, Paul Lemon and David Corner.

'That was an unhappy moment at Sunderland and so was the Jimmy Adamson era. I wasn't there long after he took over and I'm not blaming him, but the club were having a bad time and there were a lot of changes to the playing staff,' Monty added.

Another disappointment for Montgomery was not winning that elusive England cap. 'The funny thing about that match against France, when I almost played, was that Gordon Banks actually got injured the previous Saturday playing against us at Roker Park.

'No player likes to see a fellow professional injured, but I have to say that, unfortunately for me, he recovered!'

But in the main Monty has happy memories. 'We had some tremendous times at Sunderland and there's no doubt about what was the highlight — Wembley,' he says.

Huddersfield was the scene of his greatest performance and Hull the venue for his best save, but Monty has no hesitation in saying: 'We keep coming back to Wembley, but winning the F.A. Cup there has to be the pinnacle of any player's career — particularly the way we did it as a Second Division side.

That tops it. Jimmy Montgomery (fifth from the left) uses the top of the cup as a hat after his brilliant double save helped win it for Sunderland. Also celebrating are (left to right): Richie Pitt, Billy Hughes, Bobby Kerr (chaired with cup), Dennis Tueart, Dave Watson and Ian Porterfield.

'There are constant reminders of it. When F.A. Cup-ties are televised, the start of the programme features great Cup moments of the past and I keep seeing myself standing behind Bobby Kerr when he lifts the trophy.

'I've experienced both sides of the coin in the F.A. Cup. In 1964, our promotion season, we had three tremendous matches in the sixth round against the great Manchester United side who were the Cup holders at the time.

'I was knocked cold in the first match at Old Trafford, which finished 3-3 after we had led 2-0 and 3-1. The replay at Roker brought that other side of the Cup coin and was one of my worst moments.

'We were leading against Bobby Charlton, Denis Law, George Best and Co. when I sent a goal kick straight to Law, of all people, who promptly knocked it back into the net.

'That match ended 2-2 after extra time and we lost the third game on neutral ground at Huddersfield 5-1. But when you've experienced things go wrong like that goal kick, it makes you appreciate winning at Wembley all the more.'

Monty is now a supervisor at Meadowfield Sports Centre, near Durham City, and helps a well-known North-East coach, George Wardle, with the running of Notts County's Centre of Excellence for schoolboys.

But he'll always be an undisputed Sunderland Great.

MONTGOMERY'S SUNDERLAND RECORD

League appearances: 537
F.A. Cup appearances: 41
League Cup appearances: 33
European Cup-Winners' Cup appearances: 4

CHAPTER THREE

Dave Watson

As Christmas in 1970 approached, Sunderland manager Alan Brown gave the club what proved to be the ideal present. He paid out the first six-figure fee in the club's history for Rotherham United's Dave Watson.

Sunderland were short of cash at the time, gates were poor by Roker standards and results were too inconsistent for the team to be classed as genuine promotion contenders.

So the £100,000 signing of Watson was a bold move, particularly as, at the time, he was a little-known player. How that was to change!

Nottingham-born Watson had started his career as a centre half with Notts County and was snapped up by Tommy Docherty, when he was manager at Rotherham, for just £5,000.

The Doc switched Watson to centre forward, where he was used by Brown to add height to his lightweight attack. But it was in his original position that he eventually blossomed.

He was a dual-purpose player, whose ability both in defence and attack was perfectly illustrated during the glorious 1973 Cup run.

In the third round, Sunderland were drawn away to Third Division Notts County and fell behind in the 27th minute to a Les Bradd goal. That's the way it stayed until 11 minutes from time when Watson, who had been moved up front from centre half by manager Bob Stokoe just nine minutes earlier, headed the equaliser against his former club.

Dennis Tueart supplied the cross, and while the switching of Watson kept Sunderland in the Cup, they were also indebted to an important Jimmy Montgomery save which denied Bradd a second goal just prior to the equaliser.

Sunderland, who went on to unforgettable Wembley glory, had been just 11 minutes from going out of the competition at the first hurdle. Watson's goal not only kept the club in the competition, but fired immediate Cup fever on Wearside.

The replay at Roker three days later drew what was then Sunderland's biggest crowd of the season — 30,033 — and they saw Watson strike again to put his side ahead ten minutes into the second half.

Tueart added a second and Sunderland were through to meet Fourth Division Reading in the fourth round at Roker, largely through Watson's usefulness as an attacker.

Reading were managed by another of my Sunderland Greats — Charlie Hurley, who made an emotional and successful return to Roker as his side held his former club to a 1-1 draw on Wearside.

Watson played at centre half in that match, but was switched up front again for the replay at Elm Park and was the player mainly responsible for Hurley's side being blitzed in an opening 28 minutes which settled the tie.

He gave Sunderland the lead in just 80 seconds and then helped create further goals for Tueart and Bobby Kerr. Reading later pulled back a goal from the penalty spot, but a 3-1 victory meant a fifth-round tie against Manchester City at Maine Road for Stokoe's resurgent side.

Sunderland celebrated their success at Reading with champagne — a taste they were to get used to in a season which got better and better.

The signing of centre forward Vic Halom from Luton Town meant that Watson could revert to centre half again and on a permanent basis, too. It also created a settled Sunderland side, which stayed together for the remainder of that sensational Cup run.

City were beaten 3-1 in a Roker replay in front of a huge crowd of 51,782. The first meeting finished 2-2 and those

Climbing highest — and Watson usually cid.

two games were the highlight of Sunderland's run prior to the semi-final and confirmed that Stokoe's stars need fear no side.

Before that semi against Arsenal, though, Sunderland had an all-Second Division sixth-round tie on their hands against Luton, who had done the double over them in the league.

Sunderland's biggest home crowd of the season — 53,151 — saw a solid, if unspectacular performance take their side into the semi-final. They also saw once again how effective Watson was as an attacker, as well as a defender.

It was Watson who achieved the breakthrough in the 55th minute, rocketing a header home from a Bobby Kerr corner. It was his fourth — and last — goal of the Cup run, a total which made him joint top scorer for Sunderland in the magical trip to Wembley with striker Billy Hughes.

Left back Ron Guthrie scored Sunderland's second goal in a 2-0 win against a Luton side which included Viv Busby — now chief coach at Roker.

Arsenal were Sunderland's opponents in the semi-final at Hillsborough, home of Sheffield Wednesday. Just as they did against Manchester City and went on to do against Leeds, the Roker side triumphed in style against the hottest of favourites.

Halom and Hughes got the goals in a 2-1 win and so it was on to Wembley for Watson's finest hour — or hour and a half to be precise — in a Sunderland shirt.

I have no hesitation in picking that game as his best for the Roker club, because it was as near to perfection as a centre half performance could be.

I have since made a careful study of his display in a video recording of the final and Watson didn't come off second best in a single tackle. He was almost as dominant with his head, one of his great strengths through his ability to hang in the air.

Out of 20 high balls contested, the Sunderland centre half was outjumped only once.

On the ground, he won all 15 tackles and also won the ball cleanly on another three occasions with interceptions.

His display in the 1-0 victory against Leeds was rewarded with the majority of man-of-the-match awards and, fittingly and more importantly, a call-up to the England squad.

He says: 'My time at Sunderland, and 1973 in particular, was the launching pad for the rest of my career. But I could well have stayed at Roker for the rest of my playing days if we had won promotion.

'I was 29 when I left and my big regret was that I wasn't part of a Sunderland side which won promotion. I became an England player while I was there, but I wanted to play in the First Division, too.'

The match which stands out in Watson's memory from Sunderland's Wembley run is not the final, but the third round tie at Meadow Lane against his former club.

'My equaliser at Notts County was so important because we could have been out at the first hurdle. And the best game at Roker from my point of view was not during the cup run, but against Derby County the following season in the League Cup.

'We played a 2-2 draw at the Baseball Ground and the replay at Roker was also a draw — 1-1. We won the toss for home advantage in the third match and won 3-0 on a great night,' Watson recalled.

Both the serious and light-hearted sides of Watson's time at Sunderland are etched in his memory.

'Alan Brown was a big influence on me. He was a very hard man, and I learned a lot from his philosophy. He believed in physical and mental strength.

'I had that before I joined Sunderland, but he brought it out in me because I tried to be the same.

'But in contrast, there was a light-hearted side to our Cup run in '73. Billy Hughes had a laughing box and he used to switch it on when one of the lads was being interviewed on TV or in a public place.

'He even did it at the civic reception which followed our

win at Wembley. The chairman, Keith Collings, was making a thank-you speech to the Mayor when Billy went into action.

'The lads couldn't stop themselves laughing and that spirit summed up the Cup run. We did our job on the pitch, but we also enjoyed ourselves.'

Watson, in fact, found it harder going back to Wembley later in his career than he did in '73.

It became almost a second home through his England appearances, but he says: 'Perhaps it was because everything went so well against Leeds, but I worried more before matches at Wembley later in my career.

'It became harder going back, not easier. There was always the feeling that one of these days, it won't go as well on the big occasion as it did with Sunderland.'

Watson enjoys going back to Roker, but feels that the club still doesn't fulfil its potential. 'There has been too much turmoil on and off the pitch.

'A club needs continuity of management and in the boardroom, in addition to the team, if it is to be successful,' he says.

Watson spent his first two years at Roker as a centre forward. Later years were to prove that the No. 5 shirt was a better fit than the No. 9, but he still did a useful job as a regular striker.

He scored on his debut at Watford on December 19, 1970 in a 1-1 draw and his 17 league appearances for Sunderland that season brought four goals, including strikes in 'Far North' derby matches against Middlesbrough and Carlisle.

The following season, Watson was an ever-present in 47 League and Cup matches and also the club's top scorer with 14 goals.

But he was switched to centre half after three months of the next campaign by caretaker manager Billy Elliott, who was in charge between Brown's departure and Stokoe's arrival.

He had played 14 matches at the beginning of that

They shall not pass — Watson bars the way.

season as a striker without scoring, but ended it with seven goals — and an F.A. Cup-winners' medal. Watson remained with the club for another two seasons as Sunderland launched unsuccessful promotion campaigns, but he was a winner on the international stage.

The first of his 14 caps as a Second Division player with Sunderland — quite a feat in itself — was won in Lisbon against Portugal. That match, on April 3, 1974, was a goalless draw.

Playing alongside Watson at the centre of the England defence in that match was Derby County's Colin Todd, another of my Sunderland Greats. That was only Todd's second full cap and they became regular international team-mates.

Watson's understandable desire for First Division football was satisfied in the summer of 1975 when he joined Manchester City. He was valued at £275,000 with Sunderland receiving a ready-made replacement at centre half in Jeff Clarke — who continued the club's tradition for fine number fives — plus £175,000 in cash.

An England player for another seven years, Watson went on to reach 65 caps and played for another five clubs after City — Werder Bremen in West Germany, Southampton, Stoke City, Vancouver Whitecaps in Canada, and Fort Lauderdale in America.

Watson's record proves without question that he was a big success as a footballer. A similar statement can be made about his new career in business. He now runs Dave Watson International, a business and marketing consultancy. It means he is judged on results — and that was always his forte.

The National Physiotherapy Service retain him to help in the recruitment of members to their health treatment and after-care scheme. Their chief executive, Michael Bearcroft, has described him as 'our top salesman'.

Watson has all the trappings of success, including a Rolls Royce and property in Florida and Devon in addition to the family home in Nottingham, which has its own gymnasium.

Now 43, he says of his new goals: 'I get more and more ambitious all the time. It isn't greed — it's about achievement. I could leave it all behind me and laze on Mediterranean beaches for the rest of my life, but I've got used to winning. I want to keep on doing just that.'

And Dave isn't the only success story in the Watson family. His wife, Penny, is a best-selling author and company secretary and a director of a civil engineering consultancy.

Watson retains a link with international football, too. He is involved with First Artist Management, who are employed by the Football Association and the England team to handle their commercial interests.

The man who captained England four times is now a captain of industry.

WATSON'S SUNDERLAND RECORD

League appearances: 177. Goals: 27
F.A. Cup appearances: 17. Goals: 5
League Cup appearances: 7
European Cup-winners' Cup appearances: 4

CHAPTER FOUR

Dennis Tueart

On November 10, 1973, Dennis Tueart scored his first and last hat-trick for Sunderland. His goals came in a 4-1 home win against Swindon Town and the Newcastle-born winger recalls that Second Division match as his best for the club.

He also remembers it as the day he decided he wanted to leave Roker Park.

Just six months earlier, Tueart had been part of Sunderland's F.A. Cup-winning team. That success gave him a taste for the big time which he has never lost.

But it was that rather mundane league game which has stuck in Tueart's mind. 'To me, it was the perfect hat-trick. I scored with a diving header, a left-foot cracker and a tap in from a rebound, which was a scorer's goal, the type genuine finishers get.

'Yet I didn't even get the man-of-the-match award in a national newspaper which picked the top player. I started to think I wasn't appreciated. I realised that day that I had to go.

'I have nothing but love and affection for Sunderland Football Club — and that is still the case. But I had outgrown the club. I knew from my performance against Swindon what I was capable of doing and I wanted to progress.'

Tueart's split with Sunderland was not a happy one. He admits: 'From the club's point of view, it was acrimonious. The manager, Bob Stokoe, had a go at me after a match at Bristol City the week after the Swindon game.

'I admit I had a bad day. Even though I tried 100 per cent physically, I had a complete mental block in that game.'

Sunderland lost that match 2-0 and a parting of the ways

Dennis Tueart — and the shirt which said it all.

was inevitable. It was just a question of when, but it was another four months before he got his move to the First Division.

Liverpool and Derby County were two of the top clubs who wanted Tueart, but Sunderland sold him to another of the game's big boys in Manchester City. He was valued at £275,000, the club's record sale, in a deal which also took another of the Wembley winners — Micky Horswill — to Maine Road and brought Tony Towers to Roker.

City were one of the teams Tueart had helped Sunderland knock out of the F.A. Cup in the Wembley run of the previous season. That was after a memorable fifth-round replay, but he picks another replay as his best display during the glory days of '73.

That was in the fourth round, when Sunderland won 3-1 against Reading at Elm Park after a 1-1 draw at Roker, when Tueart got his side's goal.

He was also on target in the 3-1 win at Reading and says

without hesitation: 'That was my best performance in the Cup run. The final itself was not a good day for me. It wasn't my type of match — it was a nose-to-the-grindstone job for us.

'But it was still one of the three major highlights of my career and they were all at Wembley. That was the first, then there was the 1976 League Cup Final with Manchester City against Newcastle and playing there for England.

'I can remember standing on the halfway line next to Leeds' Norman Hunter when Jimmy Montgomery made his fantastic double save from Trevor Cherry and Peter Lorimer.

'Norman turned to me straight away and said, 'Your day, Dennis.' He knew then that Leeds were beaten.

'That was a special day with wonderful memories, but the overall highlight of my career has to be '76. What could top scoring a spectacular overhead winner in front of 100,000 people to win a Cup final — and to do so against your home town club?

'To start with, I felt I knew most of the crowd. I had more ticket requests from Newcastle than I did from Manchester.'

Tueart was a Newcastle fan as a lad, but says: 'They didn't come for me and Sunderland, through Charlie Ferguson, the chief scout, did. So I went to Roker.'

His league debut came on Boxing Day, 1968 against Sheffield Wednesday at Roker in a 0-0 draw. Tueart was 19 and soon established himself as a crowd favourite through his energetic style.

He made 10 First Division appearances that season, scoring against Stoke City and Wolverhampton Wanderers.

The following season saw Tueart established as a regular in a side which was relegated to the Second Division, and that's where he spent the remainder of his league career with Sunderland. It was a level at which the talented, ambitious Tueart was never going to be satisfied.

Happy days — Tueart celebrates another goal for Sunderland.

It was during those days that Tueart took to wearing distinctive white boots, which he insisted on cleaning himself rather than leaving the task to an apprentice. His sense of perfection was to rebound on him.

One Friday, he took the boots home as usual — and forgot to pack them for the following day's game!

'I didn't let on to the boss, Alan Brown. Instead, I borrowed a pair of boots from another player, Fred McIver, who was also wearing white ones at the time,' said Tueart.

'The problem was that they didn't fit me properly and it certainly affected my performance. There was no fooling the boss, either! I never made that mistake again,' he added.

After successive seasons when he scored five and four goals respectively, Tueart's strike rate suddenly improved.

In season 1971-72, he scored 13 times and the following capaign was his most successful for Sunderland in terms of goals. He hit the target 15 times, including three in the Cup run.

He would almost certainly have topped that total the following season, but for his departure to Maine Road. When he signed for City, Tueart had 14 goals to his name in 35 appearances.

They included two goals against Vasas Budapest in the European Cup-winners' Cup — the only season in which Sunderland have played in a major European competition.

His goals against the Hungarians were a brilliant solo effort in Budapest — Billy Hughes got the other in a 2-0 Sunderland win — and a penalty in the second leg at Roker, where Vasas were defeated 1-0.

Tueart's last match for Sunderland was against Portsmouth at Roker on Tuesday, March 5, 1974. The game was played in the afternoon and the attendance was only 8,142.

Three days earlier, Sunderland had played in front of 41,658 at Roker in a derby match against Middlesbrough, who won 2-0 to halt a revival which had given the club an outside chance of becoming realistic promotion challengers.

Against Pompey, Tueart signed off with two goals, including a penalty, in a 3-0 win.

Tueart's talent was not only confirmed, but developed when he left Sunderland. He won his six England caps while with Manchester City, for whom season 1975-76 was his most successful.

He was their top scorer with 24 goals, including his acrobatic winner against Newcastle at Wembley in the League Cup Final.

After two years in America playing for New York Cosmos at a time when football — or soccer as it is known in the States — was booming across the Atlantic, Tueart returned to Maine Road.

His second spell at City ended in 1983, when they were

Spectacular — Tueart scores with a flying header against Swindon. It was the day he scored a hat-trick, gave his most memorable performance for Sunderland — and decided to leave the club.

relegated to the Second Division and he went on to play briefly for Stoke City and Burnley.

In all, he made 420 Football League appearances for his four English clubs, scoring 137 goals — many of them spectacular efforts. Goals of the special category were a Tueart trademark.

Like Montgomery and Watson, who was also a team-mate with England and Manchester City, Tueart will always be remembered by Sunderland fans as being part of this F.A. Cup-winning team:

Jimmy Montgomery, Dick Malone, Ron Guthrie, Micky Horswill, Dave Watson, Richie Pitt, Bobby Kerr (captain), Billy Hughes, Vic Halom, Ian Porterfield, Dennis Tueart. Sub: David Young.

But he says: 'They weren't the only good players I played alongside during my time at Sunderland. If you picked a side from all those who were at the club during my seven years at Roker, it would be a magnificent team.

'Players like Charlie Hurley, Jim Baxter, Neil Martin and John O'Hare were on the books when I was just a kid at Sunderland.'

35

Three swells — Dennis Tueart, Billy Hughes and Ian Porterfield hit the streets of London before the 1973 F.A. Cup Final.

Off the top of his head, Tueart added: 'Imagine picking a side from a squad of Montgomery, Malone, Hurley, Watson, Colin Todd, Len Ashurst, Martin Harvey, Baxter, Porterfield, O'Hare, Suggett, Martin, George Mulhall and me.

'Sunderland always had outstanding players when I was there and my worst moments involving the club have always been when I've gone back to see a club not realising its potential.'

Tueart was ambitious and single-minded as a player. He was also a winner. He is now in business — and nothing has changed.

He runs his own company, Premier Events Ltd., a promotions and business development concern. He bought out his partner and is now based near Lymm, in Cheshire.

'My ambitions are to retain my pride and to make

We'll be running round Wembley with the cup. Tueart's lap of honour with match-winning goal scorer, Ian Porterfield.

money. I have three boys and I want to give them ambition to be successful, too. I'm not a millionaire, but it's a realistic goal,' he says.

Knowing Tueart, he will reach it.

He was involved in the TSB share flotation and kit launches for England, Liverpool and Manchester United, and Britain's Olympic teams for Seoul and Calgary.

His two years in America were, he says, the most important of his career. 'It was the best thing I've done. The States broadened my outlook on life, and taught me how football and business are closely linked.'

Tueart's new career involves the organising of travel and functions for clients. He admits: 'As a footballer, I was used to first-class travel and the best hotels.

'Now, I arrange all that. I used to be a sheep — now I'm a shepherd. Football was the first half of my life; my business is the second half.

His change of lifestyle has also brought an appreciation

of fine wine. He says: 'I was always a bit different as a player. For instance, I was probably the only sober Sunderland player on the night we won the F.A. Cup. At that time, I just didn't like alcohol.'

Tueart's involvement in football now is mainly as a fan, although he does occasionally report on matches for radio. Having settled in the North West, Manchester City are his number one club. 'Then Sunderland, with Newcastle third,' he adds.

He much prefers having a business career to the thought of staying in football as a coach or manager.

'I had natural ability as a player. Now, I have to generate it in business, but I'm still in control of my own destiny.

'That's something I wouldn't have had as a coach or manager. You're reliant on players, injuries, directors who often don't know or understand, muddy pitches and the bounce of the ball,' he says.

But he does miss the thrill of playing well in front of a big crowd in one of the country's major stadiums.

He confesses: 'If I had played well I was on such a high, I could have beaten Ben Johnson — and I wouldn't have needed drugs.

'And nothing — absolutely nothing — can compare to the thrill of scoring a goal.'

If it was a spectacular effort, that was all the better. And doing just that is how Sunderland supporters will remember Dennis Tueart.

TUEART'S SUNDERLAND RECORD

League appearances: 178. Goals: 46
F.A. Cup appearances: 17. Goals: 3
League Cup appearances: 6. Goals: 2
European Cup-winners' Cup appearances: 4. Goals: 2

CHAPTER FIVE

Len Shackleton

Just picture it. A current Sunderland player dribbles into Arsenal's penalty area at Highbury and, in a mocking gesture, sits on the ball. Just imagine a player from any side in the country, in fact, having the audacity — and ability — to do just that.

Perhaps Tottenham's £2 million signing from Newcastle, Paul Gascoigne, would be the player most likely to even think about doing it these days.

But Len Shackleton did it — one of the stories that made him a football legend. One of the reasons he became known as The Clown Prince of Soccer.

Shack wrote a book which carried that title and devoted one page to what he thought the average football club director knew about football. He left it blank — another famous Shackleton story.

He could flick a coin from his foot into the breast pocket on his jacket and bend a ball in a way which is regarded now as the exclusive right of a Brazilian.

Shack was different, a born entertainer. He was also a Sunderland Great to such an extent that, among older football fans at least, he remains the club's best-known player since the Second World War.

Leonard Francis Shackleton joined Sunderland from neighbours Newcastle on February 4, 1948 for a club record fee of £20,050. He became the star of a side which became known as the Bank of England team because of the club's spending at that time.

He replaced pre-war hero Raich Carter as Sunderland's major attraction and was soon in the scoring groove, although not with the devastating impact with which he had launched his Newcastle career.

Shack's debut for Newcastle, after signing from his home-town club Bradford Park Avenue, was against Newport County on October 5, 1946. United won 13-0, a Second Division record, and Shackleton scored six!

His first appearance for Sunderland resulted in a 5-1 defeat at Derby County, but Shack scored in the next two games, a 2-0 win against Huddersfield and a 1-1 draw against Sheffield United — both played at Roker — and ended his first season in a red and white shirt with four goals in 14 First Division matches.

The following season will always be remembered as the one in which Sunderland were humiliated in the F.A. Cup by non-league Yeovil Town, Shack being a member of the side defeated 2-1 in Somerset.

But he did come close to success in both the league and F.A. Cup during his ten years at Roker. In 1950, a shock home defeat by relegated Manchester City cost Sunderland the title and three years later they hit an unexpected decline after being impressive league leaders.

Shackleton was a regular in those Sunderland line-ups, as he was in season 1954-55 when the club were in the running for the league and cup double, but ended up missing out on both.

Sunderland lost fewer league games than anyone, but finished fourth behind champions Chelsea, Wolves and Portsmouth.

In the cup, they reached the semi-final and there was the possibility of a North East final at Wembley as Newcastle also reached that stage and the great rivals missed each other in the draw.

Sunderland had accounted for Burnley, Preston and Swansea after replays and Wolves on their way to the last four, with Shack scoring in the 3-3 draw at Preston.

But Sunderland lost 1-0 to Manchester City at Villa Park in the semi, the Roker line-up being: Fraser, Hedley, McDonald, Anderson, Daniel, Aitken, Bingham, Fleming, Purdon, Shackleton, Elliott.

Newcastle defeated York in the other semi and went on

Shack — a Roker legend.

to win the cup, no doubt increasing Sunderland's disappointment.

The following season saw Sunderland in another run to the semi-final of the F.A. Cup, knocking out the holders, Newcastle, 2-0 at St. James's Park at the quarter-final stage.

Shack missed just one match in that run, the third-round win against Norwich. He was part of the side which knocked out York and Sheffield United (after replays) and Newcastle.

Sunderland showed just one change from the side which had played in the semi-final the previous year, Bill Holden having taken over from Ted Purdon at centre forward.

But once again, there was semi-final disappointment for Sunderland, this time at Hillsborough, as Birmingham won 3-0.

The following season was Shackleton's last full campaign as a Sunderland player. He was troubled by an ankle injury and made just one appearance in the next season before retiring.

Even that, in Shack style, was handled differently, to say the least. He played in the opening game of the season against Arsenal, who won 1-0 at Roker Park in front of a crowd of 56,493. It was Alan Brown's first game as manager of Sunderland.

But the next day, Shack's column in the Sunday *Empire News* was headlined: I'VE HUNG UP MY BOOTS.

Shack revealed that he had been to see a specialist in Leeds the previous Thursday and been advised that his ankle injury would no longer stand up to football.

So Shackleton, after inspiring so many headlines, wrote his own to signal the end of a colourful career, which included a century of goals for Sunderland. His most successful season as a scorer was season 1951-52, when he hit 22 goals in 41 First Division games.

That haul included his only hat-trick for the club, Shack getting the lot in a 3-0 home win against Manchester City.

All his England caps were won while with Sunderland. He played against Wales and Denmark in 1948, Wales again the following year and, after a five-year absence from international football, returned to play against the Welsh again and West Germany.

Shack's only international goal, a typically-brilliant individual effort, came in the 3-1 victory at Wembley against World Cup holders Germany.

Strangely, Shack wasn't picked again by his country.

But his solitary goal for England is still discussed by those who feel privileged to have seen it. In fact, it seems that everyone who watched Sunderland in the 1950s has his own Shack story.

There was, for instance, the time that Sunderland, as one of the first clubs in the country to install floodlights, were playing an evening friendly match against French side Racing Club de Paris, one of a number played at that time against leading European clubs.

Racing Club had a famous centre forward, Amalfi, who

entertained the crowd before the match got underway, by demonstrating his ball-juggling skills in the centre circle.

Shack, when he saw this, immediately demanded: 'Give me a ball.' He went through his own routine and, to the delight of the Roker crowd, stole the show from Amalfi.

That was a graphic illustration of Shack's instinct to be a show stealer, something he was famed for doing when playing in London. To his opponents, it was capital punishment.

Perhaps he particularly enjoyed turning on the style at Highbury because he was rejected by Arsenal as a 17-year-old member of their groundstaff. They thought he was too small — at the time he was just 5ft. 2ins. tall — and the Gunners manager, George Allison, told him: 'Go back to Yorkshire and get a job. You'll never make the grade as a professional footballer.'

Shack grew in height and also developed to such an extent as a player that Jimmy Greaves, one of football's all-time greats, wrote in his book on outstanding goal scorers: 'Shack was a conjuror. I doubt if there has been a more skilful inside-forward in the history of British football. For Shack, the football field was a stage and he set out to give the fans entertainment even if, at times, it was at the expense of team play.

'He was nicknamed the Clown Prince of Soccer and his unpredictable, sometimes impudent play frightened the life out of the England selectors, who rewarded his incredible talent with a meagre five caps.

'Players with a tenth of his ability have won twice as many caps. The man was a genius.'

One of those rare England appearances provided Shack with what he regarded as the most memorable goal of his career — that highly acclaimed effort against West Germany.

Shack wrote: 'It was just a simple chip shot that brought me my goal, but it was special to me because it was calculated. I noted that the German goalkeeper had been coming off his line very quickly at every opportunity and had angled me well on one occasion.

'I made a mental note that if I got a similar chance, I would simply lob him. That's exactly what I did and it gave me great satisfaction to see the German goalkeeper looking back helplessly as the ball dropped over his head and into the net.'

Shack added: 'Mind you, every goal that went in for me was memorable. There's no such thing as a bad goal if you've managed to put the ball over the line.'

That's something Shackleton did for Sunderland exactly 100 times in League and Cup, a post-war record which was equalled by Gary Rowell in 1984.

I can remember Shack's mischievous humour when he was a reporter after retiring as a player. After one miserable Sunderland performance, he wrote: 'On the evidence of this display, Sunderland are certainly going places — but who wants to go to Scunthorpe!'

He also kept his Press Box colleagues amused with his instant wit. When one reporter dashed in and asked which way Sunderland were kicking, Shack immediately replied: 'Across the park.'

Needless to say, he wasn't too impressed with his former club's form at that time.

And when an opposing player placed the ball for a Sunderland player to take a free kick, Shack remarked: 'I thought he was going to show him how to kick it.'

I'll spare the embarrassment of the player concerned by not revealing his identity.

Shack, also a talented cricketer and keen golfer, was 67 this year and spends much of his retirement on the holiday island of Tenerife. It's an appropriate location for a player who presented the sunny side of football to spectators — and was often too hot for defenders.

SHACKLETON'S SUNDERLAND RECORD

League appearances: 320. Goals: 97
F.A. Cup appearances: 28. Goals: 3

CHAPTER SIX

Stan Anderson

Stan Anderson holds a unique position in North-East football as the only player to captain all three of the area's premier clubs — Sunderland, Newcastle United and Middlesbrough.

It was on Tyneside and Teesside that he tasted relative success, skippering Newcastle to promotion to the First Division in 1965 and leading Middlesbrough up from the Third Division two years later after becoming manager at Ayresome Park.

But Anderson will always be remembered mainly as a Sunderland Great due to an outstanding record of service at Roker Park which deserved a greater reward in terms of honours.

He spent 12 years on Sunderland's books and made 447 League and Cup appearances, a club record which has since been surpassed by only two players — Len Ashurst and later Jimmy Montgomery, both former team-mates.

Horden-born Anderson played for East Durham School-boys before joining Sunderland in 1951, making his league debut a year later. He soon established himself as a regular and was a rarity in the club's Bank of England team of the 1950s, as he was a home-produced player rather than an expensive signing.

Anderson made his league debut on October 4, 1952, in a 1-1 draw against Portsmouth at Roker Park. The attendance was 45,154, a regular-size crowd for Sunderland home matches at that time.

But it was the following season that Anderson established himself as a Roker regular in the number four shirt.

It was also the season in which he scored his first goals for the club, breaking his duck in a Wear-Tyne derby against Newcastle on December 19, 1953, when Anderson was Sunderland's marksman in a 1-1 draw, a match watched by a crowd of 49,922.

He was a member of the side which reached the F.A. Cup semi-final in the next two seasons, when Sunderland were defeated by Manchester City and Birmingham respectively.

And the next season was his most successful for Sunderland in terms of scoring, his 36 First Division appearances yielding seven goals.

Five of those goals came when he was playing at inside-right, rather than his usual role at right half.

The following season was one of change — and disaster — for Sunderland. They had a new manager in Alan Brown, a much-changed team and ended the campaign in a new division — the Second, for the first time in their history.

Anderson was part of a Sunderland side which cost the club their proud record of playing all their League football in the First Division. He was to spend the rest of his Sunderland career trying to lead the club back to the top flight.

The next season brought Second Division struggle, but at least Sunderland avoided a second successive relegation campaign.

By the end of that season, only Anderson and outside-left Colin Grainger remained of the side Brown had inherited.

Anderson became my first Sunderland hero in season 1959-60 when I saw my first match at Roker Park — a 2-0 win against Portsmouth.

He was already a special player in the eyes of Sunderland's supporters through his cultured wing-half displays, his forte being his superb long-range passing.

The following season saw Sunderland reach the sixth round of the F.A. Cup, an exciting run started by two

Stan Anderson — in familiar style.

Anderson goals in a 2-1 third-round victory against Arsenal at Roker Park in front of a crowd of 58,575.

Away victories in the next two rounds against Liverpool (2-0) and Norwich (1-0) took the young side led by Anderson through to the last eight and a home tie against the team who at the time were the undisputed best in the country — Tottenham Hotspur.

Welsh international winger Cliff Jones gave Spurs a flying start with a headed goal in just nine minutes, but it was a different story in the second half for the First Division leaders.

Anderson played superbly as Sunderland's pressure brought corner after corner, and 20 minutes from time, inside-left Willie McPheat equalised. Such was the noise generated by the Roker roar from a huge crowd of 61,326 that Spurs skipper Danny Blanchflower admitted that the din scared him.

An injury to Jimmy McNab saw Anderson switch from right half to left half for the replay at White Hart Lane, where Sunderland were crushed 5-0 by the brilliant Spurs side, who went on to complete the League and Cup double. The attendance in London was another massive turnout — 64,797.

The next two seasons brought heartbreak for Sunderland as they missed out on promotion in the final match on both occasions. They were also nearly men in the League Cup in the second of those campaigns.

They reached the semi-final, but were beaten 3-1 at home in the first leg by Aston Villa on a snow-covered pitch, and a 0-0 draw in the second leg was not enough.

No Sunderland player suffered more during the bitter disappointment of agonisingly failing to return to the First Division than skipper Anderson.

But at least this period brought Anderson recognition for his outstanding form with two full England caps to go with his four England Under-23 appearances from the 1950s.

Anderson's caps came in April, 1962, when he replaced Bobby Robson — now the national team manager — in the side for a 3-1 win against Austria at Wembley and a 2-0 defeat against Scotland at Hampden Park.

The England team Anderson made his international debut in was: Ron Springett, Jimmy Armfield, Ray Wilson, Anderson, Peter Swan, Ron Flowers, John Connelly, Roger Hunt, Ray Crawford, Johnny Haynes and Bobby Charlton.

Flowers (penalty), Hunt and Crawford were England's scorers and for the Scotland match, Bryan Douglas, Jimmy Greaves and Bobby Smith replaced Connelly, Hunt and Crawford.

Anderson's last season as a Sunderland player was 1963-64 and it lasted for just the first ten league games.

He was dropped after a 3-3 draw at Roker against Cardiff City, a game in which Ivor Allchurch, not for the first time, gave the Sunderland skipper a hard time.

Martin Harvey displaced Anderson and Charlie Hurley

took over as captain and led Sunderland to promotion. By then, Anderson had become a Newcastle player in a shock £19,000 deal on November 6, 1963.

He was deprived, therefore, of the satisfaction of being in the Sunderland side which restored the club to the First Division, a feat he managed with Newcastle the following season.

It's not surprising that Anderson, when looking back at his Sunderland career, selects a match from that Cup run of 1961 as his most memorable.

What is surprising is that it is not the third round win against Arsenal, when he scored Sunderland's two goals, or the sixth round tie against Tottenham. Instead, Anderson goes for the fifth-round victory against Norwich City at Carrow Road, when Charlie Hurley headed a late winner — the only goal of the game.

'I would pick that match as the most enjoyable I played in, even though it was one of those matches when we were under pressure for a long time. Despite that, I always felt we were going to win and Charlie got the winner with about eight minutes to go,' Anderson recalled.

'I enjoyed the game because we gave a team performance in every sense of the word. Everyone worked for each other and we got our reward. But from a personal point of view, I would have to say that the Arsenal game was a bit special, too,' he added.

Anderson's happiest period at Sunderland was the mid-1950s when, he says: 'It was in Bill Murray's time as manager and we should have won the First Division Championship.

'We played in two F.A. Cup semi-finals in successive seasons and one of them probably cost us the league. That was in 1955, when we were beaten by Manchester City at Villa Park and Chelsea won the Championship.

'The feeling then was that it was virtually impossible to win both the League and Cup double and the consensus of opinion was that there was more honour in going to Wembley to win the Cup.

'Now, the First Division Championship is regarded as the greatest prize in football in this country. But our priority at that time became the Cup and we eventually fell between two stools.'

Chelsea also gave Anderson his worst day as a Sunderland player, when they won 1-0 at Roker Park in the club's final match of the 1962-63 season.

'It cost us promotion, but our build-up to the game was all wrong. Everyone thought it was a formality that we would go up and there was too much celebrating in the town before the game was played,' Anderson says.

The former Sunderland wing-half selects a former team-mate, Fred Hall, as being the biggest influence on him during his time at Roker.

'Fred was like a father to me. He was a giant of a man — he must have weighed about sixteen and a half stones — and he was very domineering. I looked like a little boy when I was sitting next to him in the dressing room.

'As a young player, I was greatly influenced by what he did and said and it was a nice feeling knowing he was around to protect me. He used to say to me that if anyone battered me on the pitch I was to let him know.

'He would say, "Just let him go past you and I'll sort him out." '

Leaving Sunderland was a wrench for Anderson. 'I always felt I would be a one-club man as a player, and if things had worked out differently, that might have been the case.

'My hand was forced after I lost my place in the team in 1963. I didn't desert the club and it was certainly a strange move for a player who had been at Sunderland all his career to join Newcastle.

'So strange, in fact, that on my first day at Newcastle, I went into the visitors' room, which was what I was used to doing. But the people at Newcastle were very warm and they made me feel at home, even though I was still living in Sunderland.

'But the way things worked out, I wouldn't have changed

Anderson — in the early days.

it. When I left Newcastle for Middlesbrough, I didn't want to go, but I didn't regret that move, either.

'When I look back, I get a lot of satisfaction from the fact that I captained the North-East's three major clubs. I became regarded as a skipper during my Sunderland days and it stayed with me at both Newcastle and Middlesbrough.

'But Charlie Hurley was briefly skipper before me at Roker, then got injured. I was made captain and kept the job when Charlie returned, but I always felt it was in Alan Brown's mind to make him captain again,' Anderson said.

After managing Middlesbrough, Anderson went to Greece to coach AEK Athens and later was assistant manager at Queen's Park Rangers and the boss at Doncaster Rovers and Bolton Wanderers.

He still lives in Doncaster, but his only involvement with football now is when he scouts for friends in the game.

Football is poorer for his absence, because Stan Anderson was one of the game's gentlemen.

ANDERSON'S SUNDERLAND RECORD

League appearances: 402. Goals: 31
F.A. Cup appearances: 34. Goals: 4
League Cup appearances: 11. Goals: 0

CHAPTER SEVEN

Charlie Hurley

ON the 26th of September, 1957, Alan Brown made his first signing as manager of Sunderland. He paid £18,000 for a young centre half from Millwall called Charlie Hurley.

His debut was at Blackpool nine days later and Sunderland were slaughtered 7-0 with Hurley putting through his own goal. A week later, Sunderland were back in Lancashire and Roker fans were confident that the match couldn't go as disastrously again for their team in general and the new centre half in particular.

They were right. Sunderland were beaten 'only' 6-0 on this occasion and Hurley didn't put one past his own goalkeeper, Willie Fraser, as he had done at Bloomfield Road.

Ray Charnley, at Blackpool, and Burnley's Ray Pointer were the young centre forwards — both later to become England internationals — who gave Hurley such a torrid introduction to the First Division.

Sunderland's supporters were wondering just what Brown had seen in Hurley. Surely, he wouldn't last long at Roker. They were to find out during the next 12 years just why the manager known as The Bomber had wanted Millwall's centre half.

Hurley was to become a Wearside folk hero. He became captain of the club and also skipper of Eire, for whom he played 33 times while at Roker, and 40 in all. Sunderland haven't had a more popular or respected player.

The fact was underlined on November 25, 1979, when the club held its centenary banquet in the town's Mayfair Ballroom. At that memorable occasion, Hurley received the Supporters' Association Player of the Century award.

Hurley was an immaculate defender and prodigious header of the ball who was also, during his long and distinguished Roker career, one of the club's most feared attackers.

That was when Sunderland forced a corner and Hurley, to the expectant chant of 'Charlie, Charlie', started his trot from his defensive position to join the attack.

Corners, inevitably, were aimed high for Hurley, storming in from the edge of the box, to meet near the penalty spot. He regularly won the ball in the air and his header often produced a goal for himself or a team-mate.

A familiar picture of Hurley showed him with a black, muddy forehead, so often did he head the ball during the 90 minutes. At his peak, in the early 1960s, there wasn't a better centre half in the country.

But that was a great contrast to his miserable first season at Sunderland, which ended in relegation to the Second Division.

Hurley failed to score for his new club in 22 games in the First Division and went through the next two campaigns in the Second Division without managing to break his scoring duck.

He had to wait until his 124th League and Cup appearance for the club in his fourth season at Roker before finally hitting the target, his long-awaited goal coming in a home 1-1 draw against Sheffield United.

Hurley followed up that start by scoring two games later in a 7-1 win at Roker against Luton Town, and his third goal for Sunderland gave the club a 1-0 fifth-round win at Norwich in the F.A. Cup.

That exciting cup run didn't bring another Hurley goal, but his header from a Harry Hooper corner created Sunderland's equaliser in the quarter-final draw at Roker against mighty Spurs.

Bill Brown, Tottenham's Scotland goalkeeper, could only parry Hurley's effort and Willie McPheat made it 1-1 before the London club, en route to the League and Cup double, won the replay 5-0.

Majestic — Hurley wins another corner in the air to power in a header.

For the next two seasons, Hurley was part of a Sunderland side which reached out for the promotion prize, only to have it snatched away in the final match of both campaigns.

The great strength of the side, the engine room, was the half-back line of Stan Anderson, Hurley and Jimmy McNab.

But the following season, Anderson was displaced by Martin Harvey and moved on to neighbours Newcastle. Harvey was such a success as his successor that the new half-back line became equally effective.

Harvey, Hurley, McNab . . . the names rolled off the

tongue and that combination became one of the most successful in the country. Hurley was now established as captain and this season — 1963-64 — was the greatest of his career.

He not only led Sunderland to promotion and the sixth round of the F.A. Cup, at which stage they were finally eliminated in the third meeting with Manchester United, but finished runner-up in the Footballer of the Year voting.

It took a player of no lesser stature than West Ham's England captain Bobby Moore to prevent Hurley becoming the first player with a North-East club to win the prestigious competition organised by the Football Writers' Association.

No North-East-based player has come as close since, even though the region's teams have continued to include individuals of outstanding ability.

Hurley missed only one Second Division game that season and it was also his most successful for goals, the Sunderland No. 5 scoring seven in League and Cup.

There were joyous scenes of celebration when Sunderland defeated Charlton Athletic 2-1 at Roker to clinch promotion in the penultimate game of the season in front of a crowd of 50,827.

Hurley was carried round the pitch on the shoulders of delirious supporters, who demanded two laps of honour from a side which rivals the 1973 F.A. Cup-winning line-up as the finest Sunderland have had in my 29 years as a Roker observer.

But the champagne started to lose its sparkle in the summer when Brown resigned to take over at Sheffield Wednesday and Hurley led a managerless team back into the First Division.

It was a side also deprived through injury of inspirational goalkeeper, Jimmy Montgomery. Derek Forster, a 15-year-old boy, was in goal for Sunderland's first game back in Division One — a 3-3 draw at Roker against Leicester City — and a period of struggle and uncertainty was underway for the club.

Hurley had five seasons in the First Division after promotion was achieved and saw off the challenge to his position from Dickie Rooks and George Kinnell.

Rooks had been the regular understudy to Hurley and Kinnell was signed from Oldham for £20,000 in October, 1966. He was part of a growing Scottish clan at Roker which included the manager, Ian McColl, and Jim Baxter, who was Kinnell's cousin.

McColl succeeded George Hardwick as manager and once managed to pick three Sunderland teams for Saturday's matches at first-team, reserve and junior level, which he presented to members of his staff.

It was pointed out to McColl that he had forgotten one player . . . Charlie Hurley!

During McColl's reign, Hurley spent part of one match in goal. In season 1966-67, Montgomery was injured at Manchester United and first Hurley, then Northern Ireland international defender John Parke, who was substitute that day, took over in goal.

United's David Herd made the most of the situation, scoring against three different Sunderland 'keepers in the same match as the Old Trafford stars won 5-0.

Brown returned to manage Sunderland the following season and the next campaign was Hurley's most prolific in terms of appearances since the club's promotion.

He played in 35 League and Cup matches, but didn't score in what was his last season with the club.

Hurley's last goal for Sunderland came the previous season and, typically and appropriately, was a header in a 2-0 win at Roker against Arsenal.

Strangely, he was wearing the number four shirt at this time, which never seemed quite right for a player who was the epitome of a centre half.

He made his last appearance for the club in Lancashire, where his magnificent Roker career had started. Burnley was the venue and Hurley signed off with a win as Sunderland achieved a 2-1 success.

Of his time at Sunderand, Hurley says: 'I have wonderful

memories and to be chosen by the supporters as the player of the century was a fantastic honour, even though it was slightly unfair to the older players.

'Many of the fans who voted for me weren't old enough to see some of the club's great players.

'But I always had a special relationship with Sunderland supporters. On a home match day, we used to have lunch in the Roker Hotel then walk to the ground with the fans.

'Those were the days of 40,000 and 50,000 crowds at Roker for every game and there was no violence — at least off the pitch there wasn't!

'I had this great rapport with the crowd and they used to love to see me going up for corners. If ever I didn't, they thought I must be injured.

'I was moved to see that I have still got that relationship when I went back to the North-East 20 years after leaving, to speak at a dinner. One young man came up to me and told me that his dad still talks about me. He had heard I was ten feet tall and could jump 15 feet into the air.

'Everyone kept talking about the return of their idol and I kept turning round to see who had walked in. I couldn't believe they were all referring to me.'

Like Stan Anderson, Hurley picked the F.A. Cup fifth-round win at Norwich in 1961, when he scored the only goal, as the most memorable match of his time at Roker.

'We had only one corner and Harry Hooper, who was an artist from those situations, placed it perfectly for me. I can still picture the ball sticking in the stanchion at the back of the net,' he recalled.

But Hurley added: 'The overall highlight was winning promotion in 1964. I can still remember the scenes in Fawcett Street in the town when we were honoured at the Town Hall.

'The great thing about that team was that we all got on so well together. They were a great bunch of lads and when we meet up now it's as if we've never been apart.

'Only four of us were signings from other clubs — George Herd, Johnnie Crossan, George Mulhall and me.

The Giant — that's what Hurley was on the pitch and what he was to Sunderland's supporters.

The other seven were all products of the youth policy at the club and we had a great team spirit.'

That season, however, also produced one of the worst moments of Hurley's Sunderland days.

'It came in the sixth round of the F.A. Cup. We had three matches against Manchester United and it was terribly disappointing to go out through losing the second replay, because before that we had deserved to win.

'What made it worse for me was that, in the first match at Old Trafford, which finished 3-3, I put through my own goal. I had this little trick of knocking the ball back to the 'keeper with my head and I did it in this game, only to turn round and discover that Jimmy Montgomery was right up my backside.

'I was horrified to see the ball trickling into our net.

'But an even bigger disappointment was losing to Chelsea in the final match of the previous season, a result which cost us promotion. Tommy Docherty, the Chelsea manager, fielded a hard team that day, but we still had only ourselves to blame,' Hurley admitted.

The gentle giant born in Cork in Southern Ireland and brought up as a Cockney in London, believes the game of football is not what it was.

He says: 'I still enjoy watching it, but there isn't the same affinity between players and supporters.

'We used to walk to the ground with the crowd. Now, players drive up in Porsches — and they aren't as good these days, either.

'I prefer to be actively involved in sport rather than a spectator and my wife and I play a lot of tennis now.

'It also saddened me on my last trip to Sunderland to see the Roker end chopped in half and only 12,000 in the ground. I can remember making my comeback after injury in the reserves against South Shields, and 9,000 turned up for that game just to see how old Charlie was coming along.

'But Sunderland, without a doubt, will always be my club. And every time I get up in the morning and feel my arthritic joints, I think of Roker Park — because that's where I got them!'

As a mark of his service to the club, Hurley was given a free transfer and signed for Bolton Wanderers.

After two years at Burnden Park, he moved on to Reading, where he was manager for five years.

He is now a success in business in the south of England as sales manager for a plastics company and has no direct involvement with football, but his name will always be synonymous with Sunderland Football Club.

Hurley, who was recommended to the club by their southern scout at the time, former Millwall manager Charlie Hewitt, was the perfect case against first impressions being the best.

His first two matches for Sunderland contributed significantly to the club losing its First Division status for the first time ever. They conceded 13 goals in those games at Blackpool and Burnley — and were eventually relegated only on goal average as it was then, rather than goal difference as it is now.

But Hurley ended his Roker career as a Sunderland legend.

HURLEY'S SUNDERLAND RECORD

League appearances: 357. Goals: 23
F.A. Cup appearances: 26. Goals: 3
League Cup appearances: 17. Goals: 0

CHAPTER EIGHT

Brian Clough

He's the most colourful and controversial character in football. He's arrogant, provocative and refers to himself as 'old big head'. He's also a brilliant manager with a record to prove it. He, of course, is Brian Clough.

His reputation now is founded on his managerial success at two Midlands clubs in particular, Derby County and Nottingham Forest.

But he also had a staggering record as a goal scorer in his playing days with two North-East clubs, Middlesbrough and Sunderland. And even though he made only 74 League and Cup appearances for Roker, I had no hesitation in selecting Clough as one of my Greats.

The reason was that those games produced 63 goals — a magnificent return.

Clough was born in Middlesbrough on March 21, 1935 and started his football career with his home-town club. He scored 197 goals in 213 league appearances for Boro, a record which brought him deserved international recognition.

He was capped twice by England in 1960 and also won three Under-23 caps, one at B level, and once scored all five goals for the Football League in a 5-0 win against the Irish League.

That scoring record at Ayresome Park also persuaded Sunderland to pay their neighbours £45,000 for Clough in July, 1961.

Some Boro players were probably glad to see the back of him. While he was captain there, a group of senior players signed a round-robin which stated that they would not continue to play under him as skipper.

In control — and Brian Clough usually is.

His forthright comments in the dressingroom caused the problem. Clough later said: 'I scored goals, but Middlesbrough still didn't get results. I once scored three at Charlton and we finished up drawing 6-6. I asked the defence back in the dressingroom if they thought we might win if I got six next time!'

But Sunderland and their supporters were delighted to

D

see him arrive. Manager Alan Brown received a telephone call from chairman Syd Collings while he was on holiday in Cornwall, telling him to meet Clough on his arrival at Southampton following a Mediterranean cruise and the deal was clinched.

Clough started his Sunderland career with a goal in a 4-3 defeat at Walsall on the opening day of the 1961-62 season — and just kept on scoring.

That first season brought him 34 goals in 43 League and Cup games and five hat-tricks — against Bury, Plymouth, Swansea, Huddersfield and Walsall, the latter coming in the League Cup.

The following season, his goals return was even more impressive. The first 23 Second Division games produced 24 Clough goals, including hat-tricks at Southampton and at home to Grimsby. In the League Cup, four appearances yielded another four goals.

That Southampton match produced an unusual and amusing story. Sunderland made the long journey by air, flying to Hurn Airport, near Bournemouth.

The three-strong air crew stayed in the same hotel as the Sunderland team and also went to the match. When the players asked them after the game if they had enjoyed it, they were told they had, but that it was a pity that Southampton had won.

In fact, Sunderland won 4-2, but the air crew had been supporting the team wearing red and white, thinking it was the Roker boys, who were actually wearing white that day.

They had to change because Southampton also play in red and white stripes and, as home team, wore their normal colours.

The Sunderland players had a good laugh at that, but there was nothing to smile about at Roker on Boxing Day, 1962, when disaster struck for Clough and the club in the 24th league game of the season.

The Sunderland centre-forward tore the cruciate ligaments in his knee in a collision with Bury goalkeeper Chris Harker. The injury shattered Clough's career and cast a huge shadow over the remainder of the season for the Roker club.

Bury's centre half that day was Bob Stokoe, later to manage Sunderland. He takes up the story.

'Brian was chasing the ball as Chris raced out and I knew he was hurt when they collided and was just about to get him some attention when I saw that the referee, Kevin Howley, had awarded Sunderland a penalty.

'It was never a penalty. Brian actually went into the 'keeper, as television evidence proved. I was so annoyed at the decision that I started calling Brian every name under the sun. I knew he was injured, but I didn't know how badly.

'I can still picture Charlie Hurley taking the penalty and putting it wide of the left-hand post at the Fulwell end. To make Sunderland's day even worse, Billy Griffin pinched a goal for us and we won 1-0,' Stokoe recalled.

Sunderland missed Clough's goals, even though his replacement, Nick Sharkey, scored five in one game — a 7-1 success against Norwich. And they should still have won promotion, but blew it in the final match against Chelsea.

Clough was told his career as a player was over, but he was determined to prove everyone wrong and achieve his ambition of playing in the First Division.

He missed all the following season, but Sunderland's success in winning promotion as runners-up to Leeds United provided the opportunity for Clough to reach his Division One goal.

His determination was rewarded with a comeback against all odds and 20,000 turned up at Roker to see him re-launch his career in the reserves.

On September 2nd, 1964, he finally played in the First Division. It was Sunderland's fourth match of the season, played on a Wednesday night against West Brom, and a crowd of 52,177 witnessed Clough's return.

Clough didn't mark his fairytale comeback with a goal, but came close, being denied only by the post in a 2-2 draw.

He played in the next two games, both at Roker against Leeds and Aston Villa, and managed his one and only First Division goal against the Yorkshire side,. a header at the Fulwell end in a 3-3 draw.

Sadly, Clough was forced to admit defeat after just three games. He accepted that his knee would not stand up to the rigours of league football and retired as a player.

He was awarded a testimonial match at Roker and it attracted a crowd of 31,828 — still a Sunderland record for such a game.

Clough also asked George Hardwick, Sunderland's manager at the time, to give him a job to do. He was put in charge of the youth team and immediately demonstrated the man-management flair which was to become so distinctively evident later.

But Hardwick was sacked after just six months in charge during Sunderland's first season back in the First Division and the directors decided not to retain Clough, either.

Sunderland were in relegation trouble when Hardwick arrived, but eventually finished 15th in a 22-club First Division. He had done a good job and Clough, if he had been kept, would have done a brilliant one.

Why do I say that? Just look at his record in management. On leaving Sunderland, he became a boss for the first time at Hartlepool and created such an impression in traditionally difficult circumstances that he was snapped up by Derby County, where he started to make a national impact as a manager.

At the time of writing, he had also been in charge at Brighton, Leeds and Nottingham Forest and his honours stood at two European Cup wins, two First Division Championships, one Second Division title plus a promotion, three League Cup triumphs and one win in each of the following — the European Super Cup, the Texaco Cup, the Anglo-Scottish Cup and the Simod Cup.

Clough's managerial highs and lows have been well documented. He is rarely out of the headlines, either through his latest success or controversy.

The Sniffer — the scent of a goal and Clough was there.

But the galling, nagging thought of Sunderland supporters is one of what might have been if he had been in charge at Roker Park.

He could — and should — have been. Clough once said he would 'crawl up the M1 over broken glass to manage Sunderland'. He also described his time at Roker as the happiest of his career and his son Nigel, now one of the top centre forwards in the game, was born in the town.

But when Clough wanted Sunderland, they didn't want him. And when the club later changed its mind, it was too late. The master manager, by then, was happily domiciled in the East Midlands.

Two of his former players have been in management at Roker — Frank Clark, as assistant boss to Ken Knighton, and Alan Durban. Both admit to his influence on them and both indicated they could bring hope for the future.

Both, however, were sacked before getting the chance to complete the job they had started, or at least build on it.

Sunderland fans idolised Clough as a player. After all, he regularly scored against their greatest rivals. In three appearances for the club against Newcastle, he scored three times and, against his former employers Middlesbrough, his record was four in four.

Come to think of it, Roker fans loved him because he scored in virtually every match!

They would have worshipped him as a manager, too.

The biggest disappointment during my time observing Sunderland was that the appointment of Lawrie McMenemy, whose arrival I regarded as a masterstroke, did not lead to success.

The worst decision made by the club was not appointing Brian Clough when he wanted the job.

He was a Roker Great as a player, but I believe he would have been an even bigger success as a manager.

CLOUGH'S SUNDERLAND RECORD

League appearances: 61. Goals: 54
F.A. Cup appearances: 4. Goals: 0
League Cup appearances: 9. Goals: 9

CHAPTER NINE

Colin Todd

'Charlie Hurley was my idol. He was a majestic centre half — one of the best in the country. And while he was tremendous in the air, he wasn't just a stopper. He was a clever footballer, too.

'Charlie was what you would call a footballing centre half.'

They sound like the words of a Sunderland supporter. In fact, they are the words of a Sunderland player — and one of their Greats, too.

That tribute comes from someone who actually played alongside Hurley — Colin Todd. They are a measure of the respect in which 'King Charlie' was held at Roker Park.

But Todd was also held in the highest esteem as he, too, was one of the great defenders of his time, though completely different in style to Hurley, who stood over six feet tall and was commanding in the air.

Todd was much shorter at 5ft 9in and his game was based on tremendous pace and tackling which was timed to perfection.

Chester-le-Street was Todd's home town and he helped to put it on the football map when they reached the final of the English Schools' Trophy.

One of his team-mates in that side was Colin Suggett, who joined Sunderland at the same time as Todd and is now a coach at Newcastle.

Todd could have joined Newcastle too — straight from that outstanding grounding in schools' football.

He recalls: 'I was a Newcastle supporter as a boy and they approached me, but they were beaten to it by Sunderland's chief scout, Charlie Ferguson.

'By the time Newcastle came in, Charlie had convinced me that Roker Park was the place to go. Sunderland had a good reputation for giving young players a chance and Charlie was a great talent spotter.

'He was the first big influence on me in professional football.'

There were soon others at Roker, including Brian Clough, when he was briefly coaching Sunderland's juniors.

'Later in my career, Brian signed me twice — once for Derby and then for Nottingham Forest — so I had three spells under him and I enjoyed the experience every time.

'He has played a big part in my career and been brilliantly successful in his own in management. Everyone asks the same question: How does he do it? The answer is that he has the ability to motivate his players — get the maximum out of them. It's down to that,' says Todd.

'When I first went to Sunderland as a boy, they had just won promotion and Alan Brown was manager, but he resigned. It was Ian McColl who gave me my first-team debut, but Brown came back to the club and he was another big influence on me.

'He was a very influential manager generally within the game, but when he came back it was a difficult time for Sunderland. The club had gone stale and he sold me to Cloughie at Derby to raise money,' Todd recalled.

I can vividly recall the day Todd, then aged 22, signed for Derby in a £175,000 deal — a record sale for Sunderland at the time.

It was February 18, 1971 and I was waiting to meet Todd at Sunderland's training headquarters at Washington. I had seen him the previous day and he had kindly agreed to autograph a pile of colour photographs of himself.

I was working for a magazine at the time and we were giving the signed pictures to readers as a public relations exercise.

But that night, Clough made his move for the Sunderland defender, agreed terms and Todd travelled to the Midlands.

First again — the quicksilver Todd wins the ball.

As I waited for Todd at Washington, Brown approached me and asked who I was waiting to see. When I told him, he replied: 'He won't be here today — he's signing for Derby County.'

I was one of the first reporters to know of the transfer of the Sunderland skipper and England Under-23 international, but was more concerned about how I was going to get our photographs back!

I needn't have worried. A telephone call to Colin's wife, Jennifer, provided the welcome news that, despite the impending transfer, Todd had found the time to autograph the pictures and that they were awaiting collection at his home.

Todd says he was 'young and immature' in those days, but that certainly wasn't the case in this instance. He had shown consideration and reliability and I have always been grateful to him for that.

And while, as a player, he could have been described as young, he certainly wasn't an immature footballer.

By then, he had made 184 League and Cup appearances for Sunderland. Of those, 170 were in the league and all but 26 of them in the First Division. In those matches he had established himself as one of the outstanding defenders in the country and a certain future England international.

He had, in fact, been defending brilliantly for Sunderland against the best forwards in the country since before his 18th birthday.

Todd made his debut in the League Cup at Sheffield United on September 20, 1966. It was a second-round replay after a 1-1 draw at Roker Park and Sunderland lost 1-0.

Almost a month later, he made his next senior appearance after being the regular choice as substitute. Once again it was at Bramall Lane, home of Sheffield United, and Todd's league debut ended in a 2-0 defeat.

He says: 'It was a coincidence that my debut in the League Cup and my first match in the First Division were both against Sheffield United. And while it was disappointing to lose them both, they're the most memorable matches of my time at Sunderland.

'Not because of the way I played, but because of the fact

Closing in — Todd makes his challenge.

that I was a 17-year-old lad making his debut alongside players like Jimmy Montgomery, Martin Harvey and Scottish internationals Jim Baxter, Neil Martin, George Mulhall and George Herd.

'I was very nervous, but it was also a very exciting time

for me and one that showed that I had been right to decide to go to Sunderland. I was only 17, yet I was playing in the First Division.'

Todd found himself up against Newcastle — the club he had supported — in only his third game in the First Division.

The match was played at St. James's Park and United had Welsh international centre forward Wyn Davies making his debut. The Tyne-Wear derby attracted a bumper crowd of 58,740 and Todd showed he had the temperament for the big occasion despite his tender age.

He helped Sunderland to a 3-0 win with the goals coming from Martin, Mulhall and another Scot, John O'Hare, later also to become a team-mate at Derby.

Todd was to become accustomed to big games that season, when Sunderland had an exciting F.A. Cup run.

Brentford (5-2) and Peterborough (7-1) were swept aside at Roker in the third and fourth rounds, results which took Sunderland through to a fifth-round meeting against old rivals Leeds United.

After two 1-1 draws, Sunderland were defeated 2-1 in the second replay at Hull and, in a stormy match, had Herd and Mulhall sent off.

'I'll never forget those matches against Leeds,' said Todd, who played in all five of Sunderland's F.A. Cup games that season.

'Derby matches were always something special and because of the bitter rivalry between Sunderland and Leeds, so were games against them. I think that is why, years later, the 1973 F.A. Cup win against Leeds meant so much to Roker fans.

'Beating anyone in the final would have been special, but the fact that it was Leeds added just that bit extra as far as Sunderland supporters were concerned,' Todd added.

Todd's second season as a first-team player brought his first two goals for the club, both at home in a 3-2 defeat by Chelsea and a 2-0 win against Wolves.

He also forged his partnership with Hurley, which was to

continue the following season — Charlie's last as a Sunderland player.

Todd was to have one more full season at Sunderland, which ended in relegation after continuous struggle for the club in the First Division, and two-thirds of the way through the next season in Division Two, he was transferred to Derby.

His last appearance for Sunderland was an unhappy occasion — a 4-0 home defeat by Cardiff City.

Todd went on to play for Derby, Everton, Birmingham, Nottingham Forest and Oxford in a glittering career which also brought him 27 England caps.

All were won while with Derby, where he collected two League Championship medals.

He returned to the North East and worked as a brewery representative and hoped also to make a comeback at Roker Park.

When Sunderland were managerless following the sacking of Len Ashurst and prior to the appointment of Lawrie McMenemy in 1985, former Liverpool and England defender Emlyn Hughes wanted the Roker job and would have installed Todd as his right-hand man if he had been successful in landing the position.

But Todd did find a route back into the game and in the North East, too, when Middlesbrough manager Bruce Rioch made him his first-team coach.

Despite working for one of Sunderland's greatest rivals, Todd retains his affection for his first club.

He says: 'Sunderland were good to me and their result is still one of the first I look for.'

And the last word from this Sunderland Great is about another — former team-mate Hurley.

When recalling his Sunderland days, Todd says: 'Charlie was a big help to me when I was a kid trying to make my mark in the game. He coaxed me through games and the partnership I had with him ranks alongside the one I had with Derby's centre half, Roy McFarland, as the best I had during my career.

'But I repaid him when his career was nearing the end. I reckon I carried him then — at least a bit, anyway. I certainly did his running for him!'

What Sunderland would give now for a partnership like Hurley and Todd at the centre of the defence! Come to think of it, how many clubs wouldn't happily settle for a pairing which combined pace, power, heading ability — and skill?

TODD'S SUNDERLAND RECORD

League appearances: 170. Goals: 3
F.A. Cup appearances: 10. Goals: 0
League Cup appearances: 4. Goals: 0

CHAPTER TEN

Marco Gabbiadini

Football fans need a hero — a player they can look up to and admire for the talent that makes him special.

Sadly, there aren't as many in the game generally at the moment as there were in the past. Even one outstanding player, though, injects a spash of colour into a grey team.

Even though the Sunderland side relegated to the Third Division in 1987 did include some accomplished players, it lacked an obvious crowd hero — an idol.

If ever Sunderland needed one, it was during that humiliating first season in Division Three. Denis Smith, the new manager at the club, provided one when he signed Marco Gabbiadini.

To get Gabbiadini, Smith had to sell one of Sunderland's better players, midfield man Mark Proctor, to Sheffield Wednesday for £275,000. He spent £80,000 of that fee on the then 19-year-old striker, who was with the Roker boss's previous club, York City.

Smith was Gabbiadini's mentor and knew exactly what he was bringing to Roker Park. It didn't take him long to show the fans exactly what that was and he became an instant hit.

Special players, unless they are brilliant goalkeepers or outstanding defenders, tend to become crowd favourites if they are particularly skilful or blessed with electrifying pace and a natural ability for scoring goals.

Gabbiadini comes into the second of those categories. He's a goal-scoring speed merchant, a swashbuckling striker in the mould of Malcolm Macdonald, the former Newcastle, Arsenal and England centre forward.

He's not a Roker Great yet, but has the potential to

become one and also surpass Len Shackleton and Gary Rowell as the club's leading post-war goal scorer.

For that to happen, Sunderland will have to resist pressure to sell a player who has the qualities which have already attracted some of the most successful clubs in the country.

I am delighted that Smith and chairman Bob Murray are committed to doing just that, but to keep him, Sunderland will need to become a First Division force again, otherwise the player's own ambition could mean his departure when his contract expires.

Encouragingly, that is not until 1993, as he extended his contract by two years at the end of the 1988-89 season.

At the time of writing, therefore, Gabbiadini is happy at Sunderland and this is what Murray and Smith have told me about their attitude to the player.

Murray said: 'He's not for sale. I wouldn't let him go for £2 million. We'd be letting down our supporters if we sold Marco. It's easier to keep players than sell them and then have to replace them.

'This club has sold its best players in the past — and too cheaply at that. We believe in getting our young players on long contracts.'

Smith sums up the importance of Gabbiadini to him, let alone the club, by admitting: 'If I agreed to sell Marco, then I might as well sack myself.

'I'd be losing 20 goals a season and a player I just couldn't replace. How much is he worth? Well, people pay £1 million for a 20-goals-a-season man. But I'm not interested in what other clubs would pay. I just know that he looks great value for the £80,000 I paid for him.'

The Roker boss also admits to being Gabbiadini's harshest critic. 'He tends to daydream at times and he doesn't like the stick I give him, but he bites his tongue.

'He knows it's for his own good and he knows I give him plenty of praise when he deserves it,' Smith says.

Praise is something Gabbiadini has not been short of since arriving at Roker.

Marco Gabbiadini with the boss, Denis Smith.

In only his second match for the club, at Fulham on September 29, 1987, he scored two superb individual goals in a 2-0 win. When he also scored twice in the next two games, his popularity among Sunderland supporters was assured.

The chant of 'Ole, Ole, Marco' became the Roker crowd's battle cry as Sunderland stormed to promotion as Third Division champions.

Gabbiadini struck up an almost telepathic understanding with the experienced Eric Gates, the former Ipswich and England forward, and ended his first triumphant season at Sunderland with 22 League and Cup goals in 39 appearances.

His overall scoring tally for the season was actually 24, as he also struck twice for York before moving to Wearside.

His exciting form brought international recognition at the end of that campaign when he was selected to go to Brazil with the England Under-20 squad.

Gabbiadini's second season with Sunderland, when the club returned to the Second Division, was a stark contrast of highs and lows. And the fact that he had an inconsistent time was instrumental in the team having a similar campaign.

He proved he could get goals at a higher level, hitting 23 in League and Cup including his first hat-trick, in a 4-0 win against Ipswich.

But even that achievement was tarnished when he was sent off for striking an opponent as he celebrated his third goal in the last minute of the game. It was his second sending off of the season, the other coming at Oxford in an F.A. Cup replay defeat.

In all, he missed 11 games — seven of them through suspension. The absence of such an important player for so much of the season was clearly one of the reasons Sunderland failed to qualify for the First Division promotion play-offs.

He admitted: 'I've learned a big lesson from those

Marco Goalo — Gabbiadini shapes to shoot and is on target again.

sendings off. In both cases it was retaliation, but it was also stupidity.

'They cost me a proud record. I had never been sent off before and one of my targets had been to go through my career without being sent off.

'Now, I have got a new target. Not to get sent off again. To make sure that happens, I will have to keep a tight rein on my temper.

'There was nothing premeditated in what I did. It must be something in my nature. I've squared up to people before without taking it any further.'

Those dismissals did not prevent Gabbiadini's exciting displays and spectacular goals being rewarded with the North-East Football Writers' Association award as the region's Footballer of the Year.

On becoming the first Sunderland player to receive the

honour, Gabbiadini said: 'It was brilliant news and about time a player from our club had won it.

'It was nice to win it as a Second Division player when Newcastle and Middlesbrough, even though they were both relegated, had been playing in the First Division.

'I needed to do well to prove I wasn't a one-season wonder. I made a slow start but eventually I was pleased with my goals tally, particularly as I missed 11 games.

'I'm sure I would have scored even more if it hadn't been for missing those matches, but in one respect I was relieved that something went wrong for me.

'Everything had gone so well since joining Sunderland that I knew I would have to have a setback at some time. I was almost waiting for it and it came with the two sendings off.

'But while I've already made it clear how I feel about all that, it could have been worse. I could have suffered a really bad injury as my setback and been out of action for a long time.'

Disciplinary trouble didn't prevent Gabbiadini, who was joined at Roker by younger brother Ricardo, also signed from York, continuing to receive international recognition.

He went to Albania with the Young England squad for a European Championship match and eventually won his first cap when he played in the Under-21 tournament in Toulon in the south of France at the end of the season.

Before that, Gabbiadini joked: 'When I went to Brazil, our games were against club sides, and in Albania I was a substitute and didn't get on. So I travelled around 20,000 miles without getting a cap.'

His England selection in Toulon also removed the threat of Italy pinching him from under the nose of the country of his birth.

Through his father, Nottingham-born Gabbiadini also has an Italian qualification.

Of his Sunderland career so far, Gabbiadini says: 'It's been a great move for me. The fans have been great to me and the potential of the support here makes this a big club.

Foiled — former Sunderland goalkeeper Iain Hesford saves at the feet of Gabbiadini for Hull City.

'I'm very excited about the future. I want to get goals for Sunderland in the First Division, which is still the best league in the world in my opinion. It's more of a high-scoring league than Italy and I want to prove I can score regularly at that level, too.

'The speculation about other clubs being interested is inevitable when you're catching headlines. I don't let it affect me. If the club decided to sell me, it would be their decision.

'I'm happy and under contract to Sunderland until 1993 and there is so much to look forward to in the future.'

Sunderland supporters are hoping that Gabbiadini's future continues to be at Roker Park. Players who create excitement, in addition to scoring in excess of 20 goals a season, are a rare and precious commodity.

Power — Gabbiadini bursts through.

When I told Gabbiadini that I was devoting a chapter of this book to him, I also stressed that it didn't mean I was classing him alongside the other eight players featured. Not yet, anyway.

But if he remains a Sunderland player, continues his scoring exploits — ideally in the First Division — and his international career blossoms further, then Marco Gabbiadini will genuinely become a Sunderland Great.

GABBIADINI'S SUNDERLAND RECORD

League appearances: 70. Goals: 39
F.A. Cup appearances: 4. Goals: 0
League Cup appearances: 4. Goals: 3
Other cup appearances: 4. Goals: 3

CHAPTER ELEVEN

Stokoe's All Stars

Bob Stokoe has twice had the responsibility for Sunderland team selection. On the first occasion, it was from 1972 to '76, a four-year period in which he became the club's most successful post-war manager, winning the F.A. Cup and the Second Division Championship.

The second time was for just a month at the end of the 1986-87 season, when he was caretaker manager following the dismissal of Lawrie McMenemy.

But the hardest task he had in picking a Sunderland side was far more recently, when I asked him to select the club's best team from all their post-war players.

Stokoe admitted: 'It was a mammoth task. It was only when I sat down to do it that I realised how difficult it was going to be. There were so many outstanding players to consider.

'It would have been difficult enough to pick teams from each decade since the Second World War — sides to represent the 1940s, '50s, '60s, '70s and '80s.'

I felt Stokoe was the ideal choice for such a task as, when it came to Sunderland, he had been on both sides of the fence as an employee and also an opponent.

He had played against Sunderland and also managed teams against the club. He had also twice been manager at Roker Park and at the time I approached him, also had the title of consultant at Sunderland, a position he has since relinquished.

He therefore had a deep knowledge of the club, spanning the post-war era.

Stokoe tackled the task with typical thoroughness and came up with a fascinating line-up which, I'm sure, would provoke great debate among Sunderland supporters.

Pensive — Stokoe during his second spell as manager at Roker Park.

Stokoe's proudest moment — leading out Sunderland at Wembley. Next to him is the Leeds manager, the late Don Revie, a Sunderland player in the 1950s.

He said: 'The first thing to remember was that I was picking players to play as a team, not a collection of individuals. I therefore had to pick a balanced side and decide on a system.

'I decided to play with a sweeper, the system which is so successful at the highest level these days. The ideal man for that role was Colin Todd.

'Jimmy Montgomery would be my goalkeeper behind Toddy. Monty was one of three members of my F.A. Cup-winning team to get into the side, the others being Dave Watson and Dennis Tueart.

'Watson would be one of the two centre backs in front of the sweeper, with Charlie Hurley the other. I would then have two internationals from the 1950s on either side of them. England's Willie Watson on the right and Joe McDonald, of Scotland, on the left.

'In midfield, I went for balance again with Stan Anderson as the passer and Billy Elliott, whom no-one enjoyed playing against, as the destroyer.'

That left Stokoe with three strikers to select and he chose Len Shackleton, Trevor Ford and Dennis Tueart.

'Shack and Ford would provide goals, as their records prove, and Tueart, always a special player, had great power,' Stokoe explained.

Of the eight Roker Greats I selected for this book, Stokoe named seven for his team. The odd man out was Brian Clough.

'He didn't make it, mainly because he hardly played in the First Division. He had to be considered, of course, but I eventually picked Ford as my centre forward. He was hard to play against,' said Stokoe.

The former Sunderland boss reckoned that 'a few people would be upset at the selection of the team'.

He said: 'People like Don Revie, Ivor Broadis, Billy Bingham and Arthur Wright all came into my thoughts, as did dozens of others. There were also other candidates from our Cup-winning side, like my little general, Bobby Kerr.

'And I'm sure my good pal Dick Malone, our right back in '73, will have something to say about me not managing to find a place for him. But as I've said, it was a very difficult job.

'Pop Robson was another close contender and he would make a good choice as substitute to this team,' Stokoe added.

Of the Stokoe selections, Willie Watson and Shackleton appeared for Sunderland in both the 1940s and '50s. McDonald, Elliott and Ford were all Roker players in the '50s and Hurley and Anderson represented the club in the '50s and '60s.

Montgomery, Todd and Tueart did their Sunderland service in the '60s and '70s, while Dave Watson played for the club only in the '70s.

Only Monty didn't win a full international cap, although Todd and Tueart played for England after leaving the club.

The two Watsons, Anderson, Elliott and Shackleton were also England players, while Hurley, McDonald and Ford represented Eire, Scotland and Wales respectively.

Bob Stokoe — on his return to Roker.

Elliott won his England caps before joining Sunderland, when he was a Burnley player.

So the Stokoe side, in formation, would be:

Montgomery

Todd

Watson (W)   Hurley   Watson (D)   McDonald

Anderson   Elliott

Shackleton   Ford   Tueart

Sunderland Facts and Figures

FOOTBALL LEAGUE

SEASON	DIVISION	POSITION	POINTS
1946-47	One	9	44
1947-48	One	20	36
1948-49	One	8	43
1949-50	One	3	52
1950-51	One	12	40
1951-52	One	12	42
1952-53	One	9	43
1953-54	One	18	36
1954-55	One	4	48
1955-56	One	9	43
1956-57	One	20	32
1957-58	One	21 (R)	32
1958-59	Two	15	40
1959-60	Two	16	36
1960-61	Two	6	47
1961-62	Two	3	53
1962-63	Two	3	52
1963-64	Two	2 (P)	61
1964-65	One	15	37
1965-66	One	19	36
1966-67	One	17	36
1967-68	One	15	37
1968-69	One	17	34
1969-70	One	21 (R)	26

SEASON	DIVISION	POSITION	POINTS
1970-71	Two	13	42
1971-72	Two	5	50
1972-73	Two	6	46
1973-74	Two	6	47
1974-75	Two	4	51
1975-76	Two	1 (P)	56
1976-77	One	20 (R)	34
1977-78	Two	6	44
1978-79	Two	4	55
1979-80	Two	2 (P)	54
1980-81	One	17	35
1981-82	One	19	44
1982-83	One	16	50
1983-84	One	13	52
1984-85	One	21 (R)	40
1985-86	Two	18	50
1986-87	Two	20 (R)	48
1987-88	Three	1 (P)	93
1988-89	Two	11	63

(R) = Relegated
(P) = Promoted

F.A. CUP AND LEAGUE CUP

SEASON	F.A. CUP	LEAGUE CUP
1945-46	5th round	—
1946-47	3rd round	—
1947-48	3rd round	—
1948-49	4th round	—
1949-50	4th round	—
1950-51	6th round	—
1951-52	3rd round	—
1952-53	4th round	—
1953-54	3rd round	—
1954-55	semi-final	—
1955-56	semi-final	—
1956-57	4th round	—

SEASON	F.A. CUP	LEAGUE CUP
1957-58	3rd round	—
1958-59	3rd round	—
1959-60	3rd round	—
1960-61	6th round	2nd round
1961-62	4th round	5th round
1962-63	5th round	semi-final
1963-64	6th round	2nd round
1964-65	4th round	4th round
1965-66	3rd round	3rd round
1966-67	5th round	2nd round
1967-68	3rd round	4th round
1968-69	3rd round	2nd round
1969-70	3rd round	2nd round
1970-71	3rd round	2nd round
1971-72	4th round	2nd round
1972-73	winners	2nd round
1973-74	3rd round	3rd round
1974-75	4th round	2nd round
1975-76	6th round	2nd round
1976-77	3rd round	3rd round
1977-78	3rd round	2nd round
1978-79	4th round	2nd round
1979-80	3rd round	4th round
1980-81	3rd round	2nd round
1981-82	4th round	3rd round
1982-83	3rd round	3rd round
1983-84	4th round	3rd round
1984-85	3rd round	finalists
1985-86	4th round	2nd round
1986-87	3rd round	1st round
1987-88	2nd round	1st round
1988-89	3rd round	2nd round